No More GAMES

How to build a faithful and satisfying relationship

Gábor Mihalec

© Dr Gábor Mihalec, 2015

This book was first published in Hungarian as *Megcsalás nélkül: Hűségben és elégedetten a párkapcsolatban* ('Without Cheating: Loyalty and satisfaction in the relationship'). Hungarian edition © Kulcslyuk Kiadó.

This English edition, titled *No More Games*, is published in 2018 by Autumn House Publications (Europe) Ltd., Alma Park, Grantham, England. Copyright © Autumn House Publications (Europe) Ltd.

Translated from Hungarian by Róbert Csizmadia.

All rights reserved. No part of this publication may be reproduced in any form without prior permission from the publisher.

British Library Cataloguing in Publication Data. A catalogue record for this book is available from the British Library.

ISBN: 978-1-78665-961-3

Designed by David Bell.

Printed in Serbia.

No More
GAMES

How to build a faithful and satisfying relationship

Gábor Mihalec

Contents

A personal confession		6
1	The definition of our subject	11
2	Superficial, functional and deep	41
3	Define your relationship	51
4	Define and guard the borders of your relationship	80
5	Don't put the past aside, but put it right	97
6	Let's make it 100%	126
7	How to build an atmosphere of trust and intimacy in your marriage	144
8	Kill the parasites	166
9	Talk! Talk! Talk!	196
10	They should know better: doctors, psychologists, teachers, lawyers and priests	221
Epilogue		234
Bibliography		236

*To my wife, Dora:
my friend, my love, my companion.*

A personal confession

To write a book about infidelity is quite a risky business. It is very hard - even outright impossible - to deal with this sensitive subject in a way that would make everyone happy. I'm sure there will be quite a few who will share my views, while others will find them too liberal or too strict. Whatever your judgement will be after reading this book, if I have motivated you to think more about the subject, to consciously rethink and restate the values that will guide your relationship, I will have achieved my goal.

This book is not the impartial discourse of a therapist about a topic that is as personal to him as the frog on the biologist's dissection table. I do not plan to pass on sterile, logical information that is the essence of all the experiences of couples I have counselled throughout the years. Despite having read great books on this subject that have formed my thinking (and I will quote a few of them later), I do not plan to give you a summary of what has been written in them about infidelity. Instead of that, you will find that this book is a summary of my personal and professional experiences and values.

If, as I mentioned before, there are so many great books

about infidelity, then why write another one, you could rightly ask.

My observation is that most of the books on the market deal with infidelity as an event in the past, as a trauma that has already happened, and then try to help us move on from it. My book focuses on something else. This book is for those who have a good relationship with their partner and wish to preserve it. This book is also for those who are not in a relationship at the moment, but wish to live in a faithful relationship once they find the right partner. This book is not written about possible therapeutic interventions, but it is a preventative, educative and informative book aimed at the preservation of the good things in your relationship. I believe that a good relationship – built on mutual faithfulness and satisfaction – is not due to luck or chance, but is something that the partners work for. Therefore, in the pages that follow, I will present those helpful actions that can keep it that way.

I promised a personal tone, so let me illustrate with a story from my own life. I married Dora, my wife, in 1995. That year was very successful if I count all the weddings among my friends and acquaintances. All of us were full of hope, desires and goals, and were serious about the 'until death do us part' commitment. We were all convinced that we could rise above the failures of the previous generation, that we would do things differently and build a new relationship culture: the culture of love, care and eternal faithfulness. Then something happened that we never expected. One of our friends divorced his wife because he got to know another woman who made him see life, love and even himself differently.

I still remember how Dora and I froze upon hearing the news. After we recovered from the shock, we started to ask desperate questions: 'Is no one safe? Can we then be sure of ourselves, of each other, of our relationship? Can this happen to us too?' On that evening and during the restless nights that followed we lost our innocence. The illusion of an invincible marriage vanished once and forever. We realised that marriages may be made in heaven, but fall apart on earth!

More than two decades have passed since, and we are still happily married, having raised two wonderful children, and neither of us has had an extramarital affair. This, however, doesn't mean that we are better than others; neither that we have a guarantee that this will never happen to us. As the ancient wisdom says: 'So let the one who thinks he is standing be careful that he does not fall' (1 Corinthians 10:12, NET). We are very aware of our vulnerability - we have seen it happen in our close circle of friends.

I believe this subject can be approached only with great humility. We need to show respect to those from whom we can learn, not only because they have been married for a long time, but also because they still have vibrant, happy and loyal marriages. And we need to be humble and compassionate towards those who have experienced the struggles of infidelity in their relationship, have gone through divorce and are struggling with shame. We also owe respect to those who have experienced turbulent times but haven't allowed their relationship to break apart, but have learned from the hardships and emerged with a strengthened commitment and a better relationship.

Let us be very careful with judging! 'Whoever among you is guiltless may be the first to throw a stone at her,' Jesus once said (John 8:7, NET). If we accept that infidelity starts with a thought process then we have to admit that we are all in the same boat.

I ask you to process and judge the ideas of this book with humility, and make up your own mind based on your experiences and values.

Let's name it: fling, affair, para-relationship or what?

1 The definition of our subject

We quickly realise how elusive a concept infidelity is when we try to define it. What should we call something that we are going to analyse anyway in the pages that lie ahead? Many people don't like to use the word 'infidelity' because it sounds so negative. The term implies that the person involved in the infidelity is someone who cheats, deceives, keeps secrets, and 'plays around'. Some might feel that we shouldn't be this judgemental – that we should find a more neutral expression that doesn't carry an ethical judgement. We run, however, into the same problem with the word 'cheating'. It sounds logical that someone can only be faithful to a partner to whom the person previously promised fidelity. Does this mean that fidelity can only happen within a marriage, and that we cannot talk about it in connection with any other partnership? This also sounds problematic. The term 'adulterer' is also a negative one, and it clearly implies that the person involved has broken their marriage vow. It may seem that there is no return from the land of infidelity. But, while this might be true in many cases, there are positive examples of the opposite, where the couple have been able to integrate the lessons learned into their relationship and stay married. So, then, what shall we call this phenomenon: an affair? That term, however, suggests a longer-term relationship. If someone is having an affair, the person likely would have been in that relationship for months or even years; but what about the 'one-night stands'? Do those matter? Of course they do! Maybe we should use the term 'fling'? That would suppose a person knows where he or she is heading, and, even if the person goes off-road briefly, they can recalculate the route, as a GPS would do, and quickly move on towards the original destination. However, such definitions don't take those into account who are - so to say - heading in two different directions at the same time, and with premeditation. Naturally, we cannot forget about such people when dealing with this subject. Should we then rather adopt the ethically neutral term 'parallel relationship', or, as it is used in the modern parlance, a 'para-relationship'? I was struggling with this term. On the one hand, it looks like a good choice, as it's a neutral statement of the fact that there is an ongoing situation in which the person is participating in multiple relationships at the same time. On the other hand, something deep down in me is protesting against using this term, as I know from the first-hand experience of the couples who have sought my help how damaging this situation is for them. I am aware that many argue that we should let go of the old ideology of monogamy, and that humanity should be more open towards the 'basic biological bias towards polygamy' of humans, as it is frequently stated. I will address this later, but let me state in advance that there are as many arguments to support monogamy as there are arguments to support polygamy. There is a deep-down need in the human soul to share one's life with another human being, and it is hard to achieve this level of intimacy with multiple partners.

The best example is Kusekwa, my African classmate from the university I attended in Germany. Once I asked him how he got to know his wife, with whom he obviously had a happy marriage and was raising their six children. He started telling me a story about how his family was devastated by his decision to marry Martha. Kusekwa's father was a tribal chief and had eight wives. He spent one night per week with Kusekwa and his mother and siblings, and did the same with his other wives and children. When Kusekwa met Martha, he understood that he couldn't share the feeling he had with anybody else – he could only live in a deep relationship with one wife. This was contrary to the tribal customs and the sorcerer-guided religion they practised, and it was even contrary to their economic common sense, as in his culture women worked and men enjoyed the benefits. His father confronted Kusekwa: 'Do you know that the people despise you, so you will not be their chief and you will be forced to work all your life?' Kusekwa knew this very well, yet he chose a monogamous lifestyle, as in his heart there was no place left for any other women than Martha.

We are left with a few rare terms, like 'extradyadic relationship' (extra = outside, dyad = relationship of two persons), that express the same idea as para-relationship and are understood only by experts or really well-read individuals. Sometimes the term 'triangle relationship' is used, which has one advantage in that it indicates the connection of the participants compared to each other. However, it is a misleading term as it suggests that there are three equal partners in the game, whereas such arrangements typically end up with one person feeling betrayed at some point in the relationship.

So, at the end, I decided to stick with the term 'infidelity', aware that it is not a perfect term either, but might be the best available choice concerning the subject of the book. I wanted it to be obvious from the cover of the book what its topic would be. What would have been the chance that you would have bought a book with the title, 'A Relationship that Is Protected from Extradyadic Relationships'?

I have picked my term, but I haven't defined what I mean by it yet. However, before I formulate my definition, I think that it is important to sample what others understand by this term. I was surprised, however, at how few definitions of infidelity can be found in the professional and popular literature. Here is a short list.

According to Patton and Childs the word 'affair' describes a situation where someone starts an extramarital relationship because of the poor quality of his or her own marriage.[1] It is interesting to note that according to this definition even a hobby could amount to infidelity, and it points out that the cause of infidelity is the poor quality of the relationship.

Another definition talks about a triangle relationship and calls it an acute critical life event, which 'suggests that there has been a latent crisis that wasn't taken seriously'.[2]

A third definition approaches infidelity from the direction of the content of the relationship: '. . . any life situation is unacceptable that causes the person chronic and unbearable emotional pain and violates the person's integration, thus preventing the person from feeling valued and worthy in the relationship.'[3]

The fourth definition builds on the conflict between fidelity and infidelity. Cloude and Townsend argue that loyalty means that the spouses trust each other in every aspect – not only sexually – and that we are faithful to our partner when she or he can trust us that we would do our share of the duties and fulfil whatever promises we made. Thus, loyalty includes both physical as well as spiritual fidelity. This way infidelity can have many objects that share one common characteristic: they all come between the marriage partners.[4]

The next definition takes an interesting point of view when it emphasises that the cheater is very aware when he or she steps over an invisible boundary: 'If you think your partner would be uncomfortable watching your interaction with this person, or be upset by the confidences you've shared, the closeness is dangerous. . . . Whether or not he can admit it to himself, her husband is cheating. The proof lies in his secrecy.'[5]

In my understanding, then, infidelity is a state in which a person living in a declared relationship emotionally and/or physically gets involved with a third person for a short or long term, once or several times.

I would like to elaborate on key parts of my definition. First of all, infidelity is a process. It is not a sudden, point-like act, but rather a lengthy process. It has a prelude, after which the act happens (and this can be at a given point), and has a definite subsequent effect. Secondly, it can affect all declared forms of relationships. It can be committed not only in a marriage, but in a life partnership, even in dating. It can happen in any connection that the partners called (declared) a relationship. Thirdly, infidelity is something that may happen once or on several occasions, or last for a short time or for several years. Fourthly, it can be sexual or emotional in nature. Falling in love with a third person can constitute infidelity even if no physical intimacy happens. It is also infidelity if sexual intercourse happens without any emotional involvement. Naturally, when the participants are both emotionally and sexually involved this also constitutes infidelity. The definition serves as a glimpse into our subject that I'm about to expand and refine.

How frequent is this phenomenon?

According to a general perception of the frequency of infidelity it happens somewhere between 'it doesn't exist' and 'it happens to everyone, only they deny it'. Why do I say this? Because the phenomenon of infidelity happens in a shadow world and is burdened with shame and remorse; thus an objective assessment is impossible. All the data that is collected has to be handled and analysed cautiously. With this in mind let's look at the available numbers.

The first results that I have arrived at indicate zero prevalence: there is no such thing as infidelity. On the launch of her book, *Infidelity and What's Behind It,* I interviewed Dr Kitti Almási in front of a hundred-strong audience. At one point during the interview, she conducted a quick empirical study about how often infidelity happens in the population. She asked the audience if those who had cheated on their mate would raise a hand. The result was unanimous: no one responded. Out of that hundred-strong sample no one had committed infidelity: thus infidelity 'doesn't exist' in today's society. Interestingly enough, many people were still interested enough in the subject to come to the book launch. There seems to be a contradiction here, unless everyone in the audience had been cheated on!

Later I repeated the 'research' myself. The result really surprised me this time. On a Connect training seminar, where I was working with 65 couples, I asked the participants if anyone who had committed infidelity would stand up. I was surprised to see five men and women stand up. As I expected no one to stand, you can imagine that I was pretty embarrassed and decided not to ask that question ever again. Anyway, I got a second result for our question: out of 130 people five had committed infidelity: that is 3.85%. Now, we should figure out what this number is really telling us: that 3.85% of people cheat on their mates, or that 3.85% of people are honest? I don't know.

David Olson analysed several statistical records and concluded that the rate of infidelity among men is between 30 and 50%, while among women it is 10 to 40 percent.[6]

Hans Jellouschek, a German expert on the subject, arrives at a similar conclusion in one of his books. According to him somewhere between about half and one-third of men and women cheat on their partners. Although in the past more men committed infidelity, recently women have caught them up.[7]

Ralf Nähter, who was my classmate at university, conducted research among the readers of *Family* magazine in Germany. He sampled 1,000 people on several aspects of sexuality. In response to the question, 'Have you ever had an extramarital relationship?' 66.6% of the men answered 'never', 32.6% answered that they had only 'toyed' with the idea, 4% said 'once', and 2.8% answered 'several times'. The results were similar among women: 68.2% said 'never', 25% said they had thought about it, 4.8% said 'once', and 2% said 'several times'.[8] We must admit that the sample was not representative – because the readers of family life magazines are expected to be intentional in their relationships and, furthermore, are mostly Christians, and religion is a known protective factor against infidelity. We can state, however, that a more inclusive sample would have produced a more reliable result. Nonetheless, the numbers are still interesting, especially when viewed in correlation with other factors like sexual satisfaction. The highest sexual satisfaction (44.4 points from a possible 49) was achieved by those who had never been unfaithful, made love two or three times a week, and were open about sexuality (openly discussing sexuality and trying out new practices). The lowest satisfaction points (25.014) were produced by those who had been unfaithful at least once, made love rarely and were cautious about, or rejected any discussion of, the topic of any experimentation.[9] The result is a further argument against the position that infidelity would do good to a marriage or would energise the sexual life of a couple.

At this point I would like to add a personal observation based on my experience as a therapist: namely that, out of every ten couples I see, six will be seeking help in order to rebuild their marriage after infidelity.

At last let's have a look at some data that would add to our understanding of infidelity. As a result of 'rosy glasses' syndrome the cheater often sees the third party as a very idealised person who in every aspect surpasses their spouse. These illusions often prompt the person to leave the marriage and start a new life with the partner. I have encountered several sets of research data about how lasting these new relationships are, and in every one of them the chances of survival are less than 10%. In the case of a marriage breaking up because of a third person, out of every 100 such new relationships, between eight and nine will become successful, long-lasting and happy relationships.

So much for statistics! The numbers have revealed some facts and concealed other dynamics. For example, it doesn't matter how rarely the side effect of a medication occurs, like once in ten thousand: if you are the one who has to deal with a red rash and breathing difficulties, you will have a 100% struggle with the symptoms. Cheating works the same way. The big question is whether you can do something in order to prevent infidelity and bring your chances down to zero, or whether you are vulnerable? Let's find out!

Is one kiss infidelity?

What constitutes infidelity? Not long ago I was asked this question in a lifestyle TV show. Four women and three men of the street were busy discussing the topic. One was of the opinion that a kiss isn't infidelity, and can be done without much backlash. Others felt that a kiss is too much, but as long as there were no physical contact a date would be OK. One person suggested that infidelity happens only at the moment of intercourse, but even this could be forgiven, if it doesn't happen too often. According to this opinion, a one-night stand could be permitted every two or three years, as long as it wouldn't endanger the relationship. Then someone questioned – to my delight – why anyone with a partner would need to kiss and make love to someone else if they live in a long-term, committed relationship. If there is a partner, the person should kiss and make love with the partner. I couldn't have agreed more!

For a moment I imagined myself in each of those scenarios, and concluded that I would feel bad if Dora dated another man, or kissed him, even if she said that sex would never be an option. No! She is my wife, and dating someone else or kissing another man is not an option for her: just as dating other women is not an option for me.

When it was my turn, I started by explaining why I find it problematic when we tie infidelity to a certain act in such a concrete way. The human mind is very creative. For example, if we cannot step over a fence, we tend to find other ways to get close to the forbidden fruit behind the fence without climbing over it. Likewise, these approaches mentioned above are only excuses to get closer to infidelity:

'If we only talk, but do not kiss, this is okay.' 'If we only kiss, but don't go to bed, this is okay.' 'If I only have a fling two or three times a year, but otherwise love my wife, then our marriage is not in danger.' This is a faulty way of thinking, because it doesn't concentrate on what I could do to get the most out of my marriage, but on how far I can go without irreversibly damaging the relationship.

We see this mentality at work in most areas of human life, so it is not surprising to find it in relationships and marriages as well. For example, in the food industry we rarely find that producers have the exclusive intention to produce the healthiest, most nourishing, wholesome food. They tend rather to carefully calculate the optimum amount of additives with which to bulk their products without causing harm to the consumer and damaging their company's reputation. In the car industry the ultimate goal is not to provide the best protection, but in the name of profit to use the least amount of material (after lengthy crash testing) without putting the passengers in danger. We could continue by giving examples from the building industry and other areas as well. The point is this: if you get married, do not try to find out how far you can go without endangering your marriage. You should rather do everything in your power to get the most that you can out of your relationship.

So, what would constitute infidelity? If you have read my book called *I Do - How to build a great marriage,* you are familiar with the Sternberg triangle. Robert I. Sternberg, a professor at the University of Yale, defined love as a triangle.[10] According to his research, three aspects of love must appear in a marriage in order for it to endure. The first area of love is the physical one, passion, which includes attraction, sexual desires, and the intense urge to become one with the other person. The second characteristic concerns the feeling of belonging or intimacy, the emotional part of love. The third element of love is the cognitive side of love that helps the couple to stay together in good and bad times, which we call commitment. We need all three aspects in a marriage; otherwise the relationship becomes fragile.

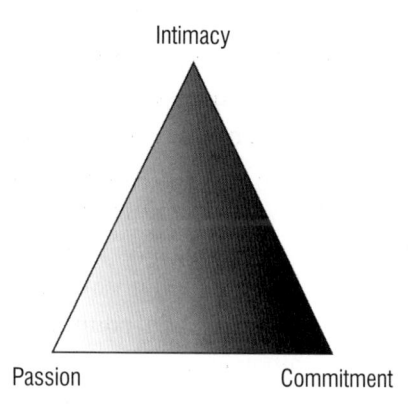

```
              Intimacy
                 △
                / \
               /   \
              /     \
             /       \
            /         \
           /_____\
        Passion      Commitment
```

Infidelity can happen in any of these three areas, and acts in each one of them can qualify fully as infidelity. Infidelity can occur in the area of passion, when a person is strongly affected by physical love that promises much greater satisfaction than any before. Or the person experiences a more liberated and sensual sexuality than they have ever experienced in their marriage (or haven't experienced for a while). The event can work as a spell that lures the person into trying to experience it again. But infidelity can happen also in the area of intimacy, when someone meets a new person and they feel as if they have known each other forever. They seem to know each other's thoughts and wishes in a magical way and can build harmony and a deep connection with each other in a very short time. It can also happen in the area of commitment, when someone becomes so important that promises made to her or him become more important than the marriage vow. The new relationship can become so strong that the person starts to experience feelings of infidelity if they are not with the new partner. The experience doesn't require sexual intimacy; it can happen purely on an intellectual level, and it becomes infidelity in the area of commitment.

In order to understand the shades of infidelity we need to have a look at John Gottman's definition of a happy and fulfilling marriage: 'Marriage isn't just about raising kids, splitting chores, and making love. It can also have a spiritual dimension that has to do with creating an inner life together – a culture rich with symbols and rituals, and appreciation for your roles and goals that link you, that lead you to understand what it means to be part of the family you have become.'[11] We can compress the couple's culture of rich inner life, rituals, symbols and inner and outer boundaries into one word: WE. In a marriage, two individuals form a new identity, a WE. Thus anything that is against this WE, anything that is only the couple's business, anything that belongs to the common sphere and is shared with a third party outside of WE, is infidelity. The infidelity definitely has an ethical side because it is an offence, and sometimes a betrayal of WE.

A conscious decision or a game of hormones?
It is a common defence after infidelity comes to light that it is not the perpetrator's fault, as the person was under the influence of hormones and couldn't direct his will. So, how does biochemistry work? What types of chemicals have an effect on our sexuality; what do they do to and in us? Let's investigate this exciting and interesting issue! Those substances that are produced in our brains as a product of sexual arousal can be categorised into two groups:

neurotransmitters and hormones. Both play an important role in how humans bond to each other.

The neurotransmitters are chemicals that transport information and are responsible for the connection between two nerve cells. The nerve cells are not in direct contact – as you might remember from your studies – but are a few microns away from each other. The gap is called the synaptic gap. The neurotransmitters are responsible for bridging this gap and carrying information from one cell into the other. It is known that depression is often caused by a low level of neurotransmitters, which is why the medication in such cases is aimed to help the production of biochemicals (for example, serotonin). During sexual intercourse our brains are literally soaked in dopamine, a powerful neurotransmitter. As a result of dopamine brain cells become more active and a positive feeling floods the body. Dopamine is often called a reward compound because its effect on the brain is similar to that of the reward candies given to pets. The acts that soak our brains in dopamine will become more and more coveted, and will exercise a really strong effect on human behaviour. However, it is important to know that dopamine is value-neutral. After something gets us excited or makes us feel good, will dopamine motivate us to repeat the act, whether it was right or wrong, potentially dangerous or harmful? The assessment of a situation, and the decision to engage in a certain behaviour or not, should not be entrusted to dopamine: it is still a job for our minds. Experiments have proved that almost all drugs that lead to addiction (alcohol, nicotine, cocaine, heroin, amphetamine and marijuana) raise the dopamine level, and this causes the individuals involved to want to relive the effect again and again.[12] Research has also proved that sex is one of the biggest dopamine generators. It has a double effect: it can excite a person to get into 'fling' relationships in order to gain sexual enjoyment (infidelity), or it can motivate a person to stick to a partner to experience again and again a wonderful sexual union (commitment between the spouses).

Now we will look into the role of hormones. There are three hormones that are especially important in sexuality: oxytocin, vasopressin and testosterone. I guess that these names are somewhat familiar, but let's take a closer look into the effects of these hormones. Oxytocin is present in both sexes, even if it is known more as a female hormone. A woman's body uses oxytocin in four different stages that are all connected to reproduction, feeding and attachment. Oxytocin production is stepped up (1) when we touch another person, and it strengthens trust and attachment; (2) during sexual intercourse, for the same reasons; (3) during orgasm and parturition in order to contract the womb; (4) during the infant's suckling of the nipples; it helps increase milk flow. It is called the neurohormone of life because it is connected to the process of passing on life and the attachment of two persons (mother/child, wife/husband).[13]

Oxytocin stimulates the areas of the brain that are responsible for attachment and trust (insula and amygdala). It can provide protection for the married partners, helping them preserve commitment and faithfulness. This is one reason why, in a good relationship, a woman experiences happiness only by seeing her partner, and it also explains why hugs and touches are important. Beware, however, for danger lurks here too! Similar to dopamine, oxytocin is also value-neutral. It cannot differentiate between good and bad, between useful and harmful; for researchers at the University of California have shown that even 20 seconds of hugging was enough for women to experience a surge in the production of oxytocin and the stir of feelings of trust and sympathy towards the men hugging them.[14] It is best to be cautious with long hugs! They might result in attachment to the person being hugged. Maybe this data should have been part of my previous discussion on why kissing and hugging a third person can constitute infidelity. Understanding the functions of oxytocin can also help explain why so many women remain in bad relationships with alcoholics or abusers.

In the brains of males, vasopressin is responsible for functions similar to those of oxytocin. Besides having important roles in regulating blood pressure and kidney functions, vasopressin has two important functions in relationships: it strengthens the attachment to the mate and to the offspring. Because of this effect it is often dubbed the 'monogamy molecule'. Male prairie voles were subjected to an experiment that tested their famous monogamous tendency. The researchers blocked the production of vasopressin in their brains, which resulted in the male voles giving up monogamy and mating with other females. However, after their brains returned to having normal levels of vasopressin they started to develop the monogamous attachments again, and showed more care for their offspring.[15] The presence of oxytocin and vasopressin raises the chances that the parents feel close to each other and cling to their children, and that the children can grow up in a family with two biological parents. However, as with the two previous chemicals, I have to point out again that this hormone is not going to force any decision into a trajectory. It is value-neutral and can serve both good and bad goals. The decision is yours.

According to Gottman, oxytocin and vasopressin play a

significant role in the formation of porn addiction, because attachments can be formed not only with a real person, but also with images, scenes, fetish objects and acts. The stronger the orgasm is, the more hormones are produced, and this process will result in a reduction of the attachment to the real partner.[16]

There is one more hormone that must be mentioned because it has become synonymous with masculinity: testosterone. Testosterone is produced in the testicles, and this in itself is expected to make a difference, compared to the other hormones, which are produced in the brain. Interestingly, testosterone can also be found in women, where it is produced by the ovaries and the adrenal glands. This hormone is responsible for the formation of male sex characteristics (hair growth, voice mutation, libido, muscles). On top of this it has important physiological roles to play in the skin, the bones, the kidneys, the liver and the central nervous system. It also influences male behaviour like aggressiveness and the 'hunting instinct'. This is why it is used to explain the need certain men have to collect trophies. This effect of testosterone is the best alibi for those men who are looking for an excuse for their infidelity. When men say that it wasn't their fault – it was in their blood – they are actually referring to testosterone. Do you remember the chorus of Gareth Gates' song called 'Stupid Mistake'? It suggests the same idea:

'Anyone of us, anyone you think of
Anyone can fall
Anyone can hurt someone they love
Hearts will break
'Cause I made a stupid mistake.'

When I was in South Africa, I kept bumping into the

memory and heritage of Nelson Mandela. At the Cape Town airport there is a large Nelson Mandela tapestry made out of beads, while in the city centre on a huge multi-storey business centre there is a portrait of him made out of glass foil. On several other buildings you can see plaques commemorating events associated with his life. On the seaside you will find his bronze statue among the other South African Nobel Prize winners. This special man spent 27 years in jail as a political prisoner because he dreamed of a country in which white and black would live in equality and with mutual respect for each other. After his release in 1994 he became the first black president of the Republic of South Africa. Many were afraid that the time of revenge had come. Here was someone who would show the whites that Africa belongs to the black people and would avenge the atrocities of apartheid. But Mandela had a very explicit answer to this expectation: 'The brain must rule over the blood!' Blood would demand revenge for those 27 lost years; it would punish a system that kept him apart from his family for so long, that took his freedom, and degraded him to a prison number. Fortunately, however, his brain had a say too – one deliberately based on higher values and greater interests – which led Mandela, or 'Madiba', as his people passionately called him, to set an authentic personal example of reconciliation for the nation to follow.

Next time, when testosterone or the hormones carry you away, and blood is rushing you into forbidden territory, remember: 'The brain must rule over the blood!' And what do you have in your brain? That's right! Oxytocin and vasopressin! So, if you want to blame the hormones, then cite those that make you more faithful to your mate, and not those that may influence you to step outside of the relationship! It is *your* choice!

A cause or a symptom?
Why do people cheat on their spouses? When a marriage breaks up after infidelity, is the cause of the divorce the third person, or is infidelity only a symptom of a deteriorating relationship, showing that there were already untreated problems in the marriage?

Infidelity can usually be traced back to three causes.[17]

1. The causes concerning the relationship.
We could summarise them as follows: the person who is expecting to receive a cake at home will surely not go to the neighbour for some dry breadcrumbs. I mention this first because the spouses have created the situation together, and as a result infidelity can be expected as a likely outcome of this downward spiral. This does not remove the responsibility of the cheater, as he or she is the person who violated the boundary of the relationship. We must acknowledge that happy, balanced and infidelity-protected marriages are the success of two persons' joint efforts; and, similarly, unhappy, unbalanced and infidelity-prone marriages are the result of the mainly unconscious actions of two persons. Put in another way we could rather talk about them being the result of idleness, neglect and misdirected efforts. In fact, the exact reasons for such failure can be numerous, but behind them lurks the general cause.

One of the most common scenarios is that, when the relationship becomes empty, the partners begin to live parallel lives, and they do not have substantive meetings any more. This state is very dangerous, as the marriage loses its strengthening, rejuvenating capacity; and, with it, its ability to protect its boundaries. The parallel lives will soon transform into parallel relationships.

Infidelity can happen in order to compensate for a deficit

of the marriage. There are relationships that work well: the spouses love each other, they are committed to each other – but they do not really find fulfilment in their sexual life. One feels it is too much, and the other feels it is too little (I will talk about this more later).

Infidelity can be a reaction to a loss of power, as when one of the partners is subservient to the other and feels that he or she has lost power. A basic relationship rule says that the partner who is less dependent on the other is the dominant one. The subordinate partner, by stepping out of the relationship, delivers a devastating blow to the power structure, and can feel less dependent as she or he begins to count on someone else. A situation like this will radically reorganise the power relations.

Infidelity can serve as a weapon to pressure the other partner in a power struggle where the person has not been able to achieve their objectives by asking, begging or quarrelling over various issues (weight loss, for example).

The goal of infidelity could also be an act of revenge prompted by a previous disappointment, offence or infidelity. In most of these cases the avenger will later regret the cheating, because the situation will sour even more.

Even though it may sound bizarre, I have even encountered a case where someone tried to bring revitalisation into the marriage by cheating. Everything was so good that it seemed boring, and something had to be done to stir up the situation. It may sound strange, but then I once read this comment in a magazine about a top model: 'I couldn't decide if she looks boringly perfect, or perfectly boring.'

2. The causes relating to the cheater.
In this situation the cheater wants to taste how others are

making the cakes. He or she knows very well how they are made at home, and might even like them that way, but is very curious to see if others make such delicious ones.

One man told me that his wife was the first and only in his life. It might sound funny, but he always had a suppressed desire to know how sex would be with someone else. As years passed by, this desire was growing stronger and resulted in pornography. At last he overcame the last barriers and started to flirt with a co-worker, only with the intention to get to know how it is to make love with another woman.

Dysfunctional family patterns can also be a driving force behind infidelity. If a person's family history reveals repeated cheating (the father cheated on the mother, and Grandma wasn't a saint either) then he or she may even unconsciously consider infidelity as a solution during a marital crisis or during a prolonged conflict.

A mid-life crisis can also cause problems, especially for men, when they start asking these questions: 'I have lived half of my life; have I achieved anything? Whatever I have experienced until now, will it help me into a more relaxed stage of life, or is there something that I am missing?' This is often the time when he wants to change the family wagon to a sports car and the wife who gave birth to three children to a more attractive, younger model.

3. The causes relating to a third person.

A woman once discreetly pulled me aside after my presentation. 'I understand that there is a cake at home, but what to do if your neighbour is a sweet shop?' Yes, this makes a point. It can happen that someone with a strong and happy marriage becomes the target of a predator. And, as history tells, even the strongest wall can cave in during a prolonged or intensive siege: especially if the besieger is extremely handsome or pretty, self-confident and novel, and exudes the promise of an incredible experience. The proactive defence of the marital border is a potent defence against this type of danger, as I will discuss later.

A fling with benefits?

Quite a number of people say, 'Why make such a fuss over infidelity? It could even be beneficial to marriage.' Let me be frank. Infidelity is not beneficial! Infidelity is a painful, damaging and alienating life event. Vansteenwegen and Luyens state: 'It is an emotional catastrophe when someone has to hear from the partner that he or she got into an extramarital relationship. . . . A world collapses in this moment. It is like losing [one's] grip on life. The pain is unbearable. It is most likely one of the biggest psychological injuries that an adult can suffer, but definitely in a relationship this is the worst experience of all. People always describe the infidelity of their partner as the worst that could happen to them, other than the loss of a child.'[18]

What about the marriages that became better after the infidelity than they were before? Yes, there are situations where infidelity has, so to say, made the marriage better, but this doesn't make the event OK. It is the victory of human consciousness if the marriage improves after the infidelity, more so than the victory of human creativity, the instinct for survival, or amazing adaptability in an emotional rollercoaster. It is, in every case, the achievement of a long and conscious process mostly supported by professional counselling. Rather than proving that infidelity is beneficial, it suggests that if infidelity happens and the couple were emotionally mature, they could learn the lesson and incorporate it into their relationship pattern – which is what post-infidelity therapy aims to do. Many a couple come to me with the distinct expectation that I should help them make their relationship just as it was before the infidelity. They are surprised to hear that I cannot accept this commission. If they were to make their relationship just as it was before the events, they would again end up in the same situation. It sounds logical, doesn't it? If they were to do everything the same way they used to, then they would simply achieve the same outcome again. Infidelity can make them aware that something has to change. The trauma can help to teach lessons that were not possible with less drastic methods. Thus the goal of post-infidelity therapy cannot be to restore the previous situation, but to incorporate the lessons learnt and to develop a new functioning relationship. It must better serve the emotional needs of the couple, and make them more aware of their need to guard the boundaries of their relationship. In this new way of relating to each other, they would be expected to feel more freedom to express their wishes, desires and needs, and to experience in a very real way the loyalty, support and solidarity of their partner.

I know a family where the husband terrorised his wife and daughters for decades. By making out that he knew everything better than anyone else, and coupling it with a raw aggression and alcoholism, he created a home climate where the tension was palpable. It so happened that this man contracted a serious illness and both his legs were amputated to save his life. In a moment the 'king' of the house became a cripple in a wheelchair in need of constant care and help. This made him rethink his life and face up to what he had done to his family for over 20 years. He called a family meeting, asked for their forgiveness and thanked them for still being loyal to him. His wife, now his widow, remembers the subsequent years as the best times of their marriage.

There were another couple who didn't have any obvious problems in life. They loved and cared for each other. The husband worked a lot in order to provide a better future for the family. (How nice work-a-holism can be made to sound!) He always considered his wife a strong woman who, beside her career, was also an exemplary housewife. He even boasted in front of his friends about his good life, how he didn't even have to wash a single plate, and that his wife never complained even when he needed to work long hours, even on Sundays. When their daughter was born the husband continued to work with the same pace, but his wife became more anxious, started to show signs of depression, and battled compulsions. Things became so bad that the husband eventually couldn't go to work, having to stay home, as the wife couldn't even provide basic care to their child. This forced the man to re-evaluate his priorities and he started to make changes to his life. He made a conscious decision to put his family first and work second. The result is that they now spend more time together, he listens to his wife more intently, and they have deeper conversations. Their life is more balanced than ever. Why? Because the depression made them rearrange their family life for the better.

What is my point with these stories of amputation and depression? Would you like to experience this for yourself just to make your life better? I guess not! Yet are there people who benefit from the calamities of life? Yes, there are.

There is one thing to recognise: not all amputations have a happy ending, like the one above, turning a bully into a good husband and father. Most would probably slide into even deeper waters. And not all depressions will automatically transform family life, making it happier and more balanced - quite the opposite! Likewise, not all marriages survive infidelity to become better afterwards than they were before. Most marriages fail, or just barely function, after infidelity happens. However, there are still miracles!

And what if it's too late for prevention?

As I mentioned before, this book is not going to focus on therapy aimed to rebuild the marriage relationship after infidelity has happened. However, I cannot go on without writing a few hopeful words to those who are struggling with the pain and despair experienced in the aftermath of infidelity.

First of all, it is true that infidelity most often leads to the breaking up of the marriage relationship, but there are a lot of opposite outcomes. Marriage can be saved after infidelity happens, and the lessons learnt can even improve its quality. This is most often the result of hard work and a well-planned and well-executed therapeutic process.

Due to the fact that the WE that binds the spouses together on a deep level suffers damage, the primary objective must be to restore this WE experience and the trust that it brings during the very vulnerable first phase of recovery. This is similar to the process of dating which results in the forming of a couple in the first place. In those days the couple had to build trust between total strangers, with whom there was no prior experience or history. That process started on zero, and, as we got to know each other, gained positive impressions and experienced each other in different situations, we started to bond and form our trust in this person we were coming to regard as trustworthy, honest, and reliable. As the rebuilding progresses it becomes easier to rely on the partner again, which in turn builds more trust. To restore trust we have to walk the same road as the courting couple, except that we are starting it from minus ten.

In this phase it is very normal for the person who was cheated on to be very suspicious, doubt the word of the partner, and demand explanations about time schedule, meetings, persons met, emails received and phone calls. The cheater in this phase must provide accountability and transparency for a transitional period. An important step in regaining lost trust is to prove his or her trustworthiness. Naturally, if this control oversteps normality and becomes compulsive and unhealthy then it needs to be discussed. Meanwhile the cheated party has to understand that he or she cannot always be beside their partner and monitor his or her every move, meeting or call. If the partner wants to cheat again, they will find the way, so there is no other option than to trust if the relationship is to be saved. This is the decision that needs to be made, even if our emotions initially rebel. It is important to know that emotions tend to follow our decisions, only with some delay. So, once you decide to trust your partner, emotions will take some time to process and follow – maybe a few days or weeks – but they will follow.

The spouses have to struggle with different challenges during the stages of recovery. They struggle when the events initially come to light; after that they struggle with the decision to carry on; sometimes they relapse; then they reach a point of new commitment and they learn to live with and trust each other.

For the cheated party, maybe the biggest challenge is to be open towards the cheater without sacrificing his or her dignity. Women especially are tempted to start competing against the rival. They start to cook their partner's favourite meals, buy and wear new lingerie, exercise to gain a better figure, go on a diet and turn on their sexual drive. This desperate attempt to gain the husband back is likely to be counterproductive. He might simply say: 'My marriage used to stumble along; my needs were not met – it didn't matter how much I asked; nothing changed. Now there are two women looking out to fulfil all my wishes. My wife is prettier than ever, has become a tiger in bed, and I have become the first and most important person in her life. With the other woman I can experience the excitement of a budding relationship, and taste the "forbidden fruit". I have never had things better!' So why would he want to change the situation? As infidelity is a problem of boundaries, with one of the partners having stepped over a border that both neglected to protect, the cheated partner must protect her boundaries with vigour. When she sacrifices her dignity, the cheater will overstep the boundaries. The challenge is to show openness towards the cheater while guarding one's dignity and even growing it. On top of this there is the grief over the broken relationship, and the ongoing struggle with a new situation.

The cheater also has to do a lot of psychological work. It takes a long time to arrive at a decision to want to restore the old relationship and end the new one. There is a great danger of relapse (just one more weekend 'to say goodbye', just one last kiss, etc.). The termination of the relationship will only be successful if it is radical and final – only that will bring proper closure. Nobody quits smoking by smoking one less cigarette every day. As long as the relationship with tobacco exists, we cannot talk about a person being tobacco free, because the addiction still exists. The cheater must let go of the hope that the budding relationship will ever bloom. He or she will most likely mourn the missed opportunity to start a promising new relationship with the third person. He or she might think that in this relationship everything would have been exciting and ideal: but in reality 90% of such relationships end within three years. In other words: if somebody gets divorced because of a new relationship, this new relationship has a 10% chance of surviving the next three years.

Finally, there is one more important step: the ethical closure. This simply means that we are to ask for forgiveness and be willing to forgive. This is easy to say, but is much harder to implement. Infidelity used to be an ethical problem; nowadays there are strong trends in our culture to relativise sin, so that people do not feel remorse after violating borders. I've heard this many times in therapy: 'I know everybody expects me to go down on my knees and ask for forgiveness. But I didn't do anything bad. I didn't kill anyone; I'm a good man; I do everything for my family!' Once a person even said, 'As I provide all finances for this family, I have the right. Yes, it did happen, and it will happen again!' With such an approach even a faint illusion of restoration must be relinquished – at least of a reciprocal, equal and developing deep relationship. Even if some type of normality returns to the relationship, the problems will resurface. Repentance has three stages, each of which must happen if a couple want to experience restoration.

1. 'I'm sorry that it came to light.'
At this stage the cheater doesn't have any remorse, but feels rather that they are suffering due to the unpleasant turn of events. He or she experiences the embarrassment of explaining what has happened to their friends; doesn't know

how to relate to the children; doesn't know what to say to the parents, etc. Emotional eruptions happen often during this stage. There is the frequent blaming of the partner who was 'spying' and of friends who 'betrayed' them. Everything that happened in the dark now comes to light and usually, after the initial shock, the person feels some relief. There is no need to lie any more; there is no secret: everybody knows about the affair, and thus it becomes quasi-legal. However, it still feels bad to look into the eyes of the partner. . . .

2. 'I'm sorry I hurt you.'
After leaving the blaming phase behind, the person starts to see further than the inconveniences of being detected. They start to see all the hurt they have caused, the shattered dreams, the faded hopes and the lost trust. They begin to feel sorry for the other person, whom they still love deep down in their heart. Anyway, the partner is still the father or mother of their children.

They find themselves saying, 'I'm sorry I hurt you!' But at the same time they may add, 'But it was good and I would do it again!' To this type of sorrow the cheated partner will react angrily. Without pointing out what is wrong with the sentence, she or he will reject it, pointing out that the apology lacks honesty and doesn't feel authentic. At this moment, behind the anger there is sadness for not hearing a genuine apology or any regret, only pity for the consequences – as, were the other able to do it without consequences, they would do it again.

3. 'I'm sorry I did it.'
This is the crucial part. The cheater can now see the real gravity and consequences of the deed. He or she can see the challenge of restoring lost trust, just how deep the damage to

the WE bond really is, and how strong the partner's emotional reactions are when they are late, or don't answer the phone. The cheater doesn't only regret causing hurt to loved ones, but also that infidelity happened at all. Seeing and experiencing first-hand the damage that their behaviour has caused, they wish they could go back in time and undo the extramarital relationship, and be more careful of the marital boundaries. It is vital for the cheater to arrive at this point, as this will determine the couple's chances of marriage restoration. It is important not only to recognise the problem, but to clearly express remorse for what has happened. The person who was cheated on then has to respond to this. Forgiving is a decision in which the person gives up the right to seek retribution against the one who has wronged them. This includes not bringing the issues up in the future or using them to 'blackmail' their partner. The partner who was cheated on will struggle emotionally with this, but in time their feelings will change in support of the decision. This is a long, hard process of the soul.

During therapy forgiveness rituals can be helpful. The parties each write out a very personal letter, one that they will read aloud. The letter contains sections about why they are thankful for each other; what the experience has taught them about each other and their marriage; their asking for and giving of forgiveness; what type of relationship they want in the future; and what they will do to protect their boundaries. After the letters are read in the protected environment of the session, we then discuss what type of emotions they have evoked. This ritual is always a big milestone – one that will serve as a reference point for the future and lay the foundation for a new life. If the infidelity was known in the wider family, then a garden party could serve as a celebration of this new beginning.

This is not an easy road: many times it is dotted with pain, and moves up and down from time to time. The restoration after infidelity will not happen overnight, just as the relationship wasn't made vulnerable in one day. The neglect and decay of the relationship developed over long years, so it is unrealistic to expect it to heal in a short time. This process could be expected to take months to complete.

Summary

Infidelity is a state in which a person living in a declared relationship gets emotionally and/or physically involved with a third person for a short or long term, once or several times. Anything that is against the WE-sense, anything that is only the couple's business or belongs to the common sphere but gets shared with a third party outside of WE, is infidelity.

[1]John Patton & Brian Childs, *Generationsübergreifende Ehe- und Familiengesorge*, p. 119. [2]Hans Jellouschek, *Warum hast du mir das angetan? Untreue als Chance*, p. 41. [3]Kitti Almási, *Hűtlenség . . . és ami mögötte van*, p. 22. [4]Henry Cloud and John Townsend, *Boundaries in Marriage*, pp. 130-135. [5]John M. Gottman & Nan Silver, *What Makes Love Last? How do I build trust and avoid betrayal?* pp. 69-70. [6]David H. Olson and John DeFrain, *Marriages & Families: Intimacy, Diversity, and Strengths*, p. 22. [7]Jellouschek, *Warum hast du mir das angetan?* p. 11. [8]Andreas Bochmann and Ralf Nähter, *Sexualität bei Christen: Wie Christen ihre Sexualität leben und was sie dabei beeinflusst*, p. 116. [9]Bochmann & Nähter, pp. 127-128. [10]Robert I. Sternberg, *Psychology of Love*, pp. 119-138. [11]John M. Gottman & Nan Silver, *The Seven Principles for Making Marriage Work*, ch. 11. [12]Joey S. McIlhaney and Freda McKissik Bush, *Hooked: New Science on How Casual Sex Is Affecting Our Children*, p. 34. [13]McIlhaney & Bush, p. 36. [14]Glen Norval & Elizabeth Marquardt, *Hooking Up, Hanging Out, and Hoping for Mr Right: College Women on Dating and Mating Today*, p. 14. [15]McIlhaney & Bush, p. 42. [16]Gottman & Silver, *What Makes Love Last?* p. 63. [17]I'm citing these causes from Alfons Vansteenvegen & Maureen Luyens, *Pedig szeretjük egymást . . . Hogyan éljük túl a félrelépést?* pp 50-60. [18]Vansteenwegen & Luyens: *Pedig szeretjük egymást . . .* , pp. 17-18.

Three types of marriages:

Superficial, functional and deep

2

I was around ten years old when, in my grandparents' street, a pedestrian pathway was built out of concrete slabs. The workers worked there for a week or so, and after they were gone my grandpa asked me to come out and see their workmanship. He directed me to have a thorough look at the pathway. 'What do you see?' he asked me. At first I didn't have a clue what to look for, but I kept looking and looking until I started to see how uneven and messy the slabs were. After telling him my observation, he stroked my hair and said: 'Remember, my son, a serious man would never do a job like this!' I understood, on that day, that his words would guide me throughout my life. How we relate to the smallest tasks and to the greatest commissions tells a great deal about the depth of our character. My grandfather was a real example for me in this. He was a simple man with little schooling, and at a mere 160cm he wasn't really physically a commanding man either. But in his work he would never compromise. He started his career as a farrier, and while still a novice he already knew how best to attach the horseshoe to the hoof. Later on he started to produce flowerpot holders out of wrought iron, tricycles for old ladies, and the moulding forms for a brick factory. Whatever he made, he wanted it to be perfect, the product of his best ability. He studied and perfected his profession in order to get the most out of himself . . . because that is how a serious man would approach his work.

Besides the fact that it feels good to reminisce, there is a point to this story. Depth can be added to marriage by studying and perfecting it. In a relationship there are also several levels of depth. We talk in everyday life about these levels, saying, for example, that this is a 'superficial relationship', that they are 'only acquaintances and not friends', or by describing someone as a 'best friend'.

I got to know a system that helps to objectively measure how deep a marriage relationship is. The Couple Checkup shows if a marriage is functional, superficial or deep, depending on which relationship type a couple is categorised into. These groups predict how successful and happy the marriage will be. The questionnaire measures a relationship based on more than 10 categories and gives an exact picture of the strengths and growth areas of the relationship. The Couple Checkup also provides a full five-factor personality diagnosis on each spouse. The unique accuracy of the online programme is guaranteed by several hundred scientifically tested questions. First the couple have to fill in data concerning their relationship type: are they dating, living together as partners, engaged or married. After this some personal data is asked for: age, cultural/ethnic background, profession, number of children. Based on the data the programme compiles a unique set of 120 questions that will help to measure the state of the relationship. After both partners have completed the questionnaire a 20-25-page evaluation is produced that gives an 'X-ray view' of the relationship. Then, with the help of a downloadable 32-page workbook, the couple can work on their relationship. This self-help programme is available on *www.couplecheckup.com* and was developed by David Olson (PhD), who has spent more than forty years refining it. The programme has been completed by at least a million couples worldwide, and Dr Olson now has the biggest research data pool on relationships.

Summary of strength and growth areas

At the beginning of the evaluation is a summary that describes how the pair are doing in the most important categories. Here is an example of this: *see Figure 1.*

Figure 1.

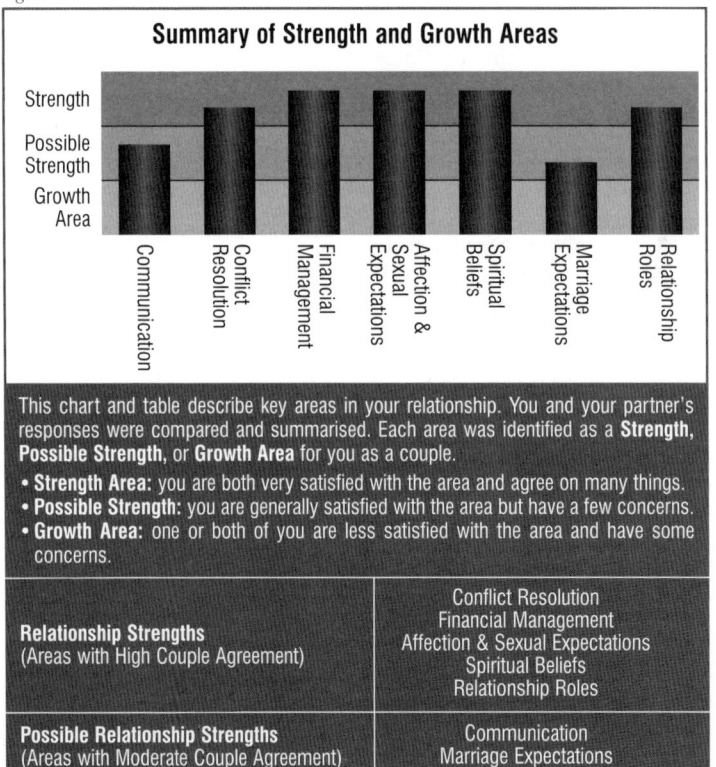

Summary of Strength and Growth Areas

Strength	
Possible Strength	
Growth Area	

Categories: Communication, Conflict Resolution, Financial Management, Affection & Sexual Expectations, Spiritual Beliefs, Marriage Expectations, Relationship Roles

This chart and table describe key areas in your relationship. You and your partner's responses were compared and summarised. Each area was identified as a **Strength, Possible Strength,** or **Growth Area** for you as a couple.

- **Strength Area:** you are both very satisfied with the area and agree on many things.
- **Possible Strength:** you are generally satisfied with the area but have a few concerns.
- **Growth Area:** one or both of you are less satisfied with the area and have some concerns.

Relationship Strengths (Areas with High Couple Agreement)	Conflict Resolution Financial Management Affection & Sexual Expectations Spiritual Beliefs Relationship Roles
Possible Relationship Strengths (Areas with Moderate Couple Agreement)	Communication Marriage Expectations

This section is followed by several pages detailing the categories for both partners. *See Figure 2.*

Communication

The **Communication** category measures how you and your partner feel about the quality and quantity of communication in your relationship. It explores how you share feelings and understanding, and listen to one another.

Individual Results for Communication

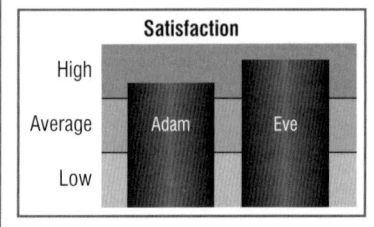

Satisfaction — Adam: Average; Eve: High

- As individuals, you are both very positive about the quality and quantity of communication in your relationship.

Couple Results for Communication

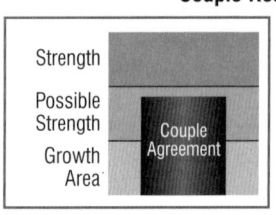

Couple Agreement: Possible Strength

Agreement Items: You both feel positive about:
- Feeling understood.
- The ability to share negative feelings.
- Whether or not you refuse to discuss problems.
- Your satisfaction with how you talk to each other.

Discussion Items: You both feel positive about:
- Feeling listened to.
- The ability to ask what you want.
- Your willingness to share feelings.

Figure 2.

This is the way information is processed throughout the programme.

The next section involves personality diagnostics, during which the individual personality traits of the partners are described and their effect on the relationship is evaluated. This is how it appears in the programme. *See Figure 3.*

Let's now focus on our topic for this chapter. The questionnaire categorises the couple's relationship into five personality types that correspond to five different levels of

SCOPE Personality Scale – Social

[Bar chart comparing Adam and Eve across five dimensions: Social (S), Change (C), Organised (O), Pleasing (P), Emotionally Steady (E), with values rated Low, Average, or High.]

The Personality SCOPE consists of five dimensions based on the Five-Factor Model of Personality.

The five dimensions, and your scores on them, are described below. Review your results on all five dimensions rather than focusing on just one or two traits where you scored high or low.

Then, as a couple, compare where your Personality SCOPE results are similar and where they are different. Discuss the advantages and potential drawbacks to each.

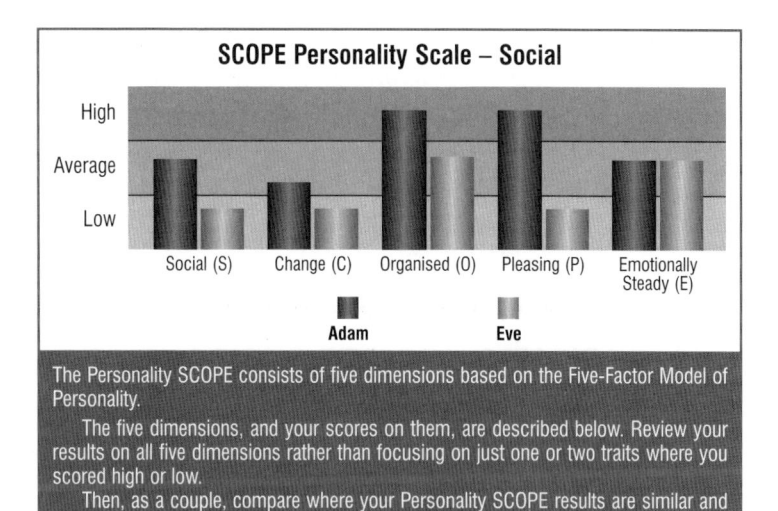

Figure 3.

relationship depth. Couple Checkup identifies these levels as: devitalised, conflicted, conventional, harmonious, vitalised. For the sake of simplicity I will group these categories into three groups in this book and describe marriage relationships as **superficial** (devitalised and conflicted types), **functional** (conventional) and **deep** (harmonious and vitalised). We will now have a closer look at these types of marriage relationships.

The superficial marriage

Couples living in this type of marriage are unhappy, and it shows. They are dissatisfied with most areas of their marriage, they have very few strengths (if any), and most of them (73-90%) are thinking about getting divorced. For years most of these couples have been stuck in a conflict situation that they cannot resolve and reach closure in by themselves. According to numerous research studies, if these couples do not make joint efforts to strengthen their marriage they will end up divorcing.[1] Even if they have some strengths, they show low scores in the interpersonal areas of their relationship, like communication or conflict resolution. The usual map of a couple in a superficial relationship looks like this: *see Figure 4.*

Figure 4.

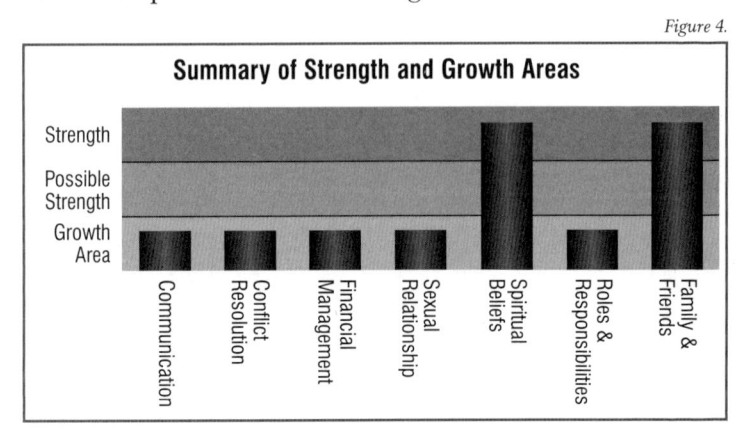

Summary of Strength and Growth Areas

- Communication
- Conflict Resolution
- Financial Management
- Sexual Relationship
- Spiritual Beliefs
- Roles & Responsibilities
- Family & Friends

However, I often meet the following pattern in couple therapy sessions: *see Figure 5.*

The quality of their relationship is the source of sadness and distress, and it eventually forces them to seek therapy.

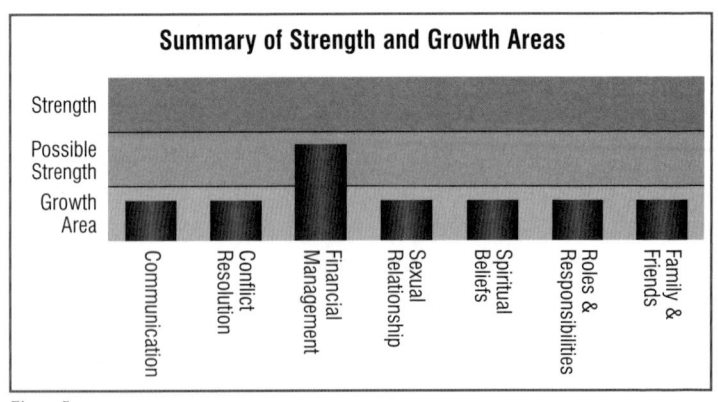

Summary of Strength and Growth Areas

- Communication
- Conflict Resolution
- Financial Management
- Sexual Relationship
- Spiritual Beliefs
- Roles & Responsibilities
- Family & Friends

Figure 5.

Most of them have never learned what it takes to make a relationship work; they didn't have a good relationship model to follow, and started their joint adventure with the notion that if they love each other everything will be just fine. Their relationship is very vulnerable and extramarital partners keep appearing, which makes a closer emotional relationship even harder to build. However, once they both have a desire to co-operate in order to build a better relationship, and they are ready for change, they will experience substantial positive change. For this to work they will need to be determined and serious about it.

The functional marriage

Functional couples may look average at first glance. They are parenting their children well; they attend the parents' meetings; they have a balanced financial situation, paying their bills on time and responsibly managing their loans. They are often deeply spiritual, having grown up in traditional religious families. They appear satisfied with life in general and about their relationship in particular; however, they have a haunting feeling that something is missing. Everything seems just so functional. Everything is working, but there is no spark in their eyes when they look at each other. Everything is working, but in an emotionally sterile environment. These couples are strong in traditional areas (spirituality, finances, parenting, family roles), but they do not do well in interpersonal areas (communication, conflict resolution, sexuality). A typical functioning pair's relationship map looks something like this: *see Figure 6.*

These couples are less likely to divorce than the superficial ones, but not because they feel so great about their marriage; rather, because they have learned to stick together even though they are unhappy. They rarely have

Summary of Strength and Growth Areas

Strength / Possible Strength / Growth Area

Communication | Conflict Resolution | Financial Management | Sexual Relationship | Spiritual Beliefs | Roles & Responsibilities | Family & Friends

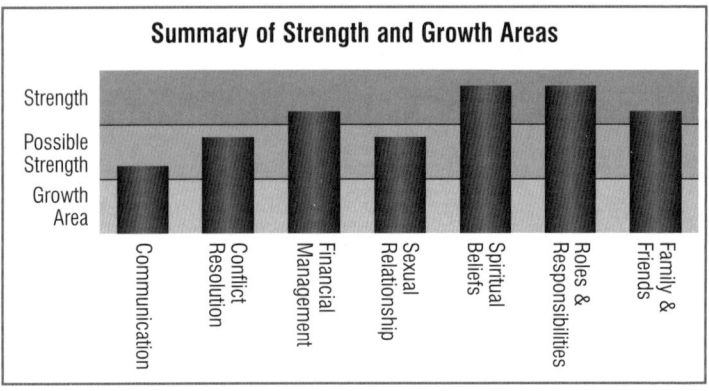

Figure 6.

problems with infidelity, but if it does happen they will experience guilt and go through an emotional crisis. They are less aware that they need help, but once they attend therapy they will do very well.

A deep marriage

These couples work on their relationships just as a serious person – so my grandfather said – would do a proper job on the pavement. Couple Checkup calls them 'harmonious' or 'vitalised' couples. As the term suggests, these couples are really lively. They consciously build and guard their relationships, and you can see this in their priorities. They radiate happiness and satisfaction, and everyone would like to be like them. They have many strengths, and even if some areas are lower they are aware of these and work on them. They guard the boundaries of their relationship against infiltrators, because in their eyes their relationship is something valuable and is to be protected. It happens only very rarely that a person in such a relationship succumbs to external infidelity, and the divorce rates are very low among them. The couples map of those living in a deep relationship looks something like this: *see Figure 7.*

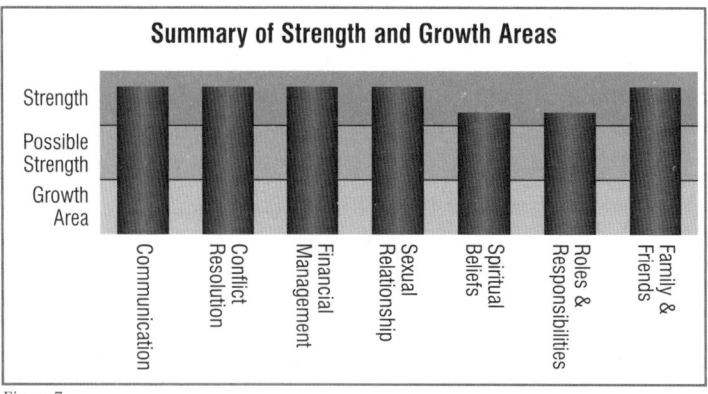

Summary of Strength and Growth Areas

- Strength
- Possible Strength
- Growth Area

Categories: Communication, Conflict Resolution, Financial Management, Sexual Relationship, Spiritual Beliefs, Roles & Responsibilities, Family & Friends

Figure 7.

For summary purposes: the existence of a deep relationship is not dependent on the choice of a good partner; nor is it just a matter of luck: but it is the result of conscientious, dedicated work. In this book I will give you many suggestions on how to become a couple like this. If this category is not the one that you recognise in your relationship, then it is time to switch into that 'calculating new route' mode, because, despite failures and bad statistics, it is possible to live happily with the same person for decades. One of my clients referred to a Rubik's cube, saying: 'Marriage is like a Rubik's cube. For sure, you can solve it, but most do not know how. There are those who do not give up and find a solution by practising a lot. Others would just give it up and stop working on it. One thing is sure, however: you can do it!'

Test your relationship!

What type of relationship do you live in? If you want to have an exact evaluation of the depth of your relationship – to get feedback about the quality of the various areas of your relationship – then take a break from reading this book and visit *www.couplecheckup.com* to fill out a Couple Checkup. I'm sure that you will then read the rest of the book with heightened interest. Anyway, to fill out a Couple Checkup is great to do as a form of 'compulsory marital maintenance'. We – Dora and I – fill out one every two years to see where we are in our relationship. This is a time for us to celebrate our strengths, and to commit again to work on our growth areas.

Never be satisfied with a mediocre relationship! Just as you can choose to do the paving job well, so you can choose to enjoy a marriage lived at the deepest levels of intimacy.

[1] Blaine J. Fowers, Kelly H. Montel & David H. Olson, 'Predicting Marital Success For Premarital Couple Types Based on PREPARE', *Journal of Marital & Family Therapy*, 1996/22/1, pp. 103-119.

Taking steps towards a cheatproof marriage

3 Define your relationship

A couple in their fifties are sitting in front of me. Their surnames differ from each other, and when they introduced themselves they didn't specify the nature of their relationship. As we talk, it becomes clear that they love each other, but in some respects they act as if they are not committed to each other, while in others they talk as if their relationship functioned according to declared rules. So eventually I asked them the question: 'Would you tell me who you are to each other?'

Suddenly they become tense: they look at each other, then at me again; then the woman nods at the man as if to tell him to speak first. He is obviously embarrassed, searches for the right words, then suddenly spells out the most exact answer: 'We actually are living in an undefined relationship.'

I guess he couldn't have been more precise. How could anyone provide a fulfilling, deepening relationship that provides emotional safety to his or her partner if they haven't defined their relationship? Yet many live without ever asking this question of themselves or their partner. Their relationship doesn't have a goal to grow towards: they simply live beside each other. However, they do have expectations from the relationship and from the partner.

This is why this couple asked for help when they got stranded in their relationship.

It is useful to know in the different stages of the relationship where we are, what we can expect from the other partner, what we should put into the relationship and what its valid rules are. When we start looking for a partner, our radars are calibrated on a wide spectrum. We recognise everybody who could be of interest to us, and are likely to be considering several potential partners. Then we start to concentrate on a single person. If we decide to go for a long-term relationship and we both develop the intention to get to know each other on a deeper level, then we put the others aside and start to concentrate on each other. This doesn't mean that we delete the memory of others, but it does mean that we will not initiate contact, simply because there is now someone in whom we have started to invest more. This is critical, because if we maintain several relationships parallel to each other then we reduce the chances of getting to know one person on a deeper level. This stage requires that I must treat the other person as if she or he will ultimately be the only one, otherwise he or she will never become the only one.

Then, as I'm more and more convinced that I want to share the rest of my life with that person, I will make an explicit move – I will make my intentions public. In a traditional setting this move is called engagement. This is not a finite decision, but it is a public declaration of intentions: we are serious about our relationship and we want this relationship to move towards mutual commitment and exclusivity. If the time spent together before this moment didn't give enough assurance that the person is the one you want to spend the rest of your life with, then you should move on and reactivate all the names you still have stored in your memory. Naturally, it can happen that someone else comes into the picture that hasn't made the list before. Anyway, the process restarts, and in the case of mutual interest and growing commitment we will again put all the other persons aside, and zoom in again on the one person that we want to know better and deeper. When we find the person we would like to be with, we are faced with a very definite decision. A joint journey starts, one that we want to walk together and only with each other. This is called marriage. Once we arrive at this stage, we delete other possible partners for good from our memory. From this moment on we will focus exclusively on one person. The moment of entering into marriage is very well described by Professor Maria Kopp and husband Árpád Skrabski: 'What is the essence of becoming married? This is a public show of commitment that closes the life stage of seeking for a partner, and it is witnessed by those who are closest to us. Rites play a significant role in the organisation of human society. It is not by chance that someone becomes a medical doctor the moment the person receives the diploma. The same way, when people refuse the marriage rituals they are protesting against accepting their identity formed by the closing of the search period. It is a global phenomenon that the formation of identity is becoming longer, and the identity quest of teenage years is dragging on for decades. This is true for career choice and also for choosing a mate.'[1]

The marriage ceremony is a significant milestone. It closes the stage of searching and starts a new stage. On the wedding day I declare in front of everybody that I've stopped searching. Leaving the search phase behind, I now step into the 'I've found it' phase.

There are two events in my relationship with Dora that I

remember very well, events that signalled that I had narrowed my search. We were engaged, but still about half a year from the wedding. I was working in a watch shop as a salesman, and one particularly pretty girl started to visit the shop frequently. Every time she came, she asked me to help her to put a watch on her wrist in order to see whether it fitted, but she never bought one. When I was putting on a watch on her wrist for the umpteenth time I realised that she was holding her hand in such a way that it would make contact with mine. At that moment I realised why she came so frequently to the shop: she wanted to make contact and build a relationship. At this moment a red light started to blink and the alarm bell started to ring in my heart: the intruder alarm! Someone was threatening my relationship with Dora! My brain sent a command to my fingers and forced them to drum on the desktop showcase, so that my ring knocked noisily on the glass. When she saw my ring she became a bit embarrassed, said goodbye, left and never returned.

The other situation was when I was looking for something in my wallet and found a condom that I had put into a hidden compartment quite a while before. I guess at school you also heard this type of advice during those sex education sessions: 'Always have a condom on hand; you never know when you'll need it!' When I found this condom I was already married to Dora. As I stood there with this condom in my hand it dawned on me that I already had someone special! So why did I have a condom in my wallet 'just in case'? Anyway, what does 'just in case' mean in my present situation? I remember thinking about this dilemma: if I leave the condom in my wallet, that means that I am consciously leaving open the possibility that I might cheat on Dora – worse still, I was giving myself permission to do so! If I threw away the condom, that would mean that if I ever got into a situation where I might need it, I wouldn't have it. What was I to do? On that day I made a decision that was at least as important as my 'I do!' in front of the registrar and the minister. I told myself: 'I have a wife, and I do not want to – I cannot – get into a situation with another woman in which I would need this condom. My life is my choice, and it cannot be determined by circumstances or the wants of another person – only by me.'

It really dawned on me on that day what it means to take responsibility for my wife and for our relationship. On that day, I closed the door in front of others and narrowed my interest on my wife. How did Professor Kopp put it into words? Leaving the search phase behind, I step into the 'I've found it' phase. For a married man the phase of searching closes down. He will not search any more; neither is he available. Marriage and marriage rituals are designed to facilitate this closure, but the internal process doesn't finish on the wedding day for many. The change in the status is a conscientious choice. For me it was the 'condom in the wallet' situation that forced me to make this choice wholeheartedly.

This takes me to the case of two university students who decided to move in together, as this made financial sense. They only had to pay rent for one flat. They believed that their relationship was solid and interpreted this move as the right step towards a common future. However, there was a very kind girl with beautiful black hair who was sitting next to the boy on the Wednesday evening Sociology course. After they left the classroom, they often stopped in front of the building to chat for a while. At first they were just good friends; then the relationship became more intimate – until one morning when the young man woke up in his classmate's bedroom. His girlfriend was upset and hurt, but when she challenged him, he replied: 'I haven't promised anything! We were dating but I haven't committed myself to you. If I had, I would have married you!' What happened here? What I wrote about at the beginning of this chapter: the couple lived in an undefined relationship. They never articulated who they were to each other, nor what rules they would live by in their relationship. The man believed that it was a transitional situation that left several options open to him, while the woman believed that it was an exclusive relationship into which no other person had a right to step. So the best way to avoid such complications is to define the relationship. But be careful! The legal status of the relationship might not be matched by the necessary psychological maturity required by that stage. I have seen many marriages where the dynamics followed the patterns of undefined relationships, despite being legal marriages. I have also seen partnerships that were fully defined relationships, where the partners knew the rules and knew exactly what they could expect from each other. Marriage is a great opportunity, or should I say the best opportunity, to define the framework: but a framework cannot substitute for the content. The content is produced by the couple.

Who are we to each other?
- **If you are dating then say:** 'We consider ourselves a dating couple and we have the goal to discover and to get to know each other more in order to be able to decide how to continue.'
- **If you are engaged then say:** 'We are an engaged couple who have made a decision that we want to continue life together, even if we cannot fully implement our decision at this point in time.'

- **If you are living in a partnership then say:** 'We are partners who want to enjoy each other's company without commitment. We love each other and we share the good and bad in our lives, but we keep some areas for ourselves.' It is also important to discuss whether you intend to stay together for a short time or for a long term.
- **If you are married then say:** 'We are a married couple, and we have committed ourselves to a long-term, monogamous relationship where we open up all areas of our lives to each other; we will show trust and loyalty to each other and continuously work together on a shared life journey.'

So the first question we have to answer is: who are we to each other? But the second one is equally important: what are the terms of our contract?

A couple in their forties are sitting in front of me: the wife with red eyes, the husband tensely waiting for the right moment to leave the room. When I ask them what brought them into my office, the wife looks at the husband and says: 'You should say it. It is because of you that we are here!' The husband tells me that his wife has just got to know that he had an affair with a woman who used to work for their company for two and a half years. And he doesn't understand why this is such a big deal, because his wife always knew that he had affairs and that this was normal in their relationship. The wife protests angrily at this moment: 'Yes, I always knew about your girlfriends, but you never said that you were "in love" with any of them before!'

Finding her comment very strange, I asked her to clarify it: 'Am I correct in understanding that you have agreed that it is OK in your marriage if one of you goes to bed with someone else, as long as you don't fall in love with them?'

The wife gets embarrassed and starts to explain: 'No, we never had an agreement on this, and I don't want him to go to bed with other women. But the fact that he went to bed with others didn't hurt as much as him saying that he is now in love with someone else!' You should have seen the expression on the husband's face. He was very surprised to hear that his wife was hurt because of his fling relationships.

There must be a rulebook in every relationship that categorises behaviours as either acceptable or unacceptable. Even if we don't set up the rules, our behaviour and actions will inadvertently create an unspoken rulebook. Because the man always cheated on his wife, and the wife accepted the situation, the rule of their marriage became that the man could go to bed with anyone, but couldn't get emotionally attached to her. And now that something contrary was being said the husband was really surprised.

What do we include in our contract? By the way, when I mention a contract, do not think of a written document that you frame and hang on the wall of your bedroom. This contract is a simple conversation where you clarify where the red lines in your relationship are: what is acceptable to you and what you are not willing to tolerate. This agreement is very important at every stage of your relationship. Even if you haven't made a commitment, discussion of this contract can be really useful. I know a couple where the woman was convinced that sexual fidelity could be expected only after the wedding, and until then everybody was free to do whatever they liked. She acted on this principle and got into a sexual relationship with an ex-classmate just two months before the wedding. After her fiancé got to know what had happened, she told him that it didn't matter, because the wedding would annul all that had happened before, and they would start their life together on a clean sheet. They barely salvaged their relationship and the wedding, but as you could predict infidelity became an issue again ten years later. If you already live together and are committed to each other then it is even more urgent to clarify the rules: 'Did we sign up to anything when we started our life together? If we did, do we want to keep these original rules in effect, or do we want to change some rules? If not, do we make some right now that are valid for the future?' At the end of this chapter you can find an exercise that can help you word your agreement.

A short history of the culture of marriage
I would feel that something is missing from this chapter without an explanation of why people in our present society have such differing views about marriage and relationships. While for some it is obvious and self-explanatory that an extramarital affair is harmful for marriage, others want an explanation as to why they should miss the opportunity to have an affair. However, no man is an island, so let us take a look at the cultural and historical influences that have shaped our thinking about intimate relationships.

Enlightenment
Enlightenment as an historical process replaced the disciplinary and regulatory power of religion with social consensus. Before Enlightenment the medieval church ruled basically every aspect of human life, even those it had no right to, and not even the Reformation changed this. This explains the source and intentions of the Enlightenment movement, which eventually steered aspects of human life into unintended directions.

Marriage always had a ritual and sacred aspect. The couples who loved each other (or were chosen for each other by their parents) had always appeared before a priest, rabbi, guru or shaman (who represented a transcendent power) to make their commitment to each other in the presence, and with the help, of the supernatural. In the Bible's Creation story it was the Creator Himself who bound the first couple together in marriage. This symbolised that marriage is not a human institution, but a creation of the Intelligent Designer who created humanity. Thus, the spouses are not only responsible to each other, but are also accountable to God, who gifted them with the potential for marriage. Since the Enlightenment many now interpret intimate relationships within a totally different framework. The marriage is no longer a gift given from above, in which we are accountable to others, but a social creation and contract that regulates the relationship of the partners. This has also changed our terminology of right and wrong. In the previous world view right and wrong were determined by a higher power, thus making them always valid and independent of social consent, life situations or individual preferences. This was basically the concept of morality. However, the Enlightenment relativised morals, and its norms became defined by social consensus. This is why, after the Enlightenment, certain populations could be hunted down, locked up into concentration camps and executed. However, soon after that it became the social consensus that to deny the Holocaust was not socially acceptable. Morality used to be derived from a source that was above humanity, and that articulated right and wrong from an external point of view. Social consensus, however, is based on the prevailing human conception of things, changes all the time and is heavily influenced by both individual and short-term interests.

The Enlightenment has led also to the separation of religious and civil marriage. In all the countries of Europe marriage was once a privilege granted by the church, and this was accepted and guarded by state laws. The ecclesiastical nature of marriage prevailed up until the nineteenth century. The transfer of the right to conduct marriage from the priests to the representatives of society wasn't just a formal change, but it was driven by the changing ethical judgement of marriage. In a morals-based system the marriage ceremony is solemnised by an oath or a set of vows, while in a system of social consensus we talk about a marriage contract. A contract remains in effect until its validity is mutually set aside, but a vow is valid 'until death do us part'. It is interesting to observe how this difference plays out in the wording of religious and civil marriage formulas.

In a religious ceremony we may hear something like this: 'I, X, take you, Y, to be my husband/wife. I promise to be true to you in good times and in bad, in sickness and in health, for richer and for poorer. And, forsaking all others, I will love you and honour you all the days of my life. So help me God!'

While in a civil ceremony it may sound more like this: Registrar/Minister: 'Are you, X, free lawfully to marry Y?' Man/Woman: 'I am.' Or like this: 'I call upon these persons here present to witness that I, X, do take you, Y, to be my lawfully wedded wife/husband.'

In the religious ritual the partners promise to be faithful even under difficult circumstances, and they promise exclusivity and perseverance in their relationship to each other – where no other person has a right to be. They also declare that they intend to have a lasting relationship and plan to maintain it, not only in their own strength, but also by using the resources of Someone stronger and greater than themselves. In contrast, the civil wedding 'vow' omits all these references and limits its scope to the present will of the partners. What marriage means is not defined, but it delegates its content to the jurisdiction of the couple. Under such circumstances you get as many interpretations about the meaning of marriage as there are couples who marry. All couples are free to interpret what marriage means to them and to form their own marriage culture. There are no rules and restrictions or moral obligations or traditions to follow. The freedom gained can also backfire. Within the traditional concept of marriage most people knew what their task was and what they could expect in a happy marriage. The new approach leaves room for interpretation and important and helpful directions are lost, not to mention the difference between right and wrong. This concept can be seen in the modern marriage laws that are based on social consensus. The law penalises abuse as one of the worst forms of offence inside marriage, but have you ever heard a court (in Europe) penalise anyone who caused emotional distress by being unfaithful, or for failing to provide their spouse with an acceptable quality of life over a prolonged period of time? It is an interesting modern phenomenon that on the one hand some would like to prevent Peter from playing with cars, as this would predestine him to become a man, while on the other hand allow him to become male or female, despite his biological sex. These rules of modernity seem to blur so many of those guidelines that have helped orient life for ages. A culmination of this confusion is the phenomenon of Conchita Wurst, who came to international attention after winning the 2014 Eurovision song contest.

I do not want to call into question the positive changes that the Enlightenment brought with it; neither do I want to explain away or absolve the sins committed in the name of religion by religious persons. And I definitely do not want to withdraw the right of the civil marriage registrars to validate marriages. I am simply attempting to make the point that in order to use freedom in its fullness we need to have a set of clues that guide us into true freedom, and not into chaos.

Evolution

The Enlightenment proved to be a fertile environment in which to discuss and criticise faith-based values and statements. The theory of Charles Darwin about the origin of species was born in this intellectual environment. According to Darwin's view, the Earth and the lifeforms on it are not the creations of an intelligent designer, but are the products of a long evolutionary process of small changes over millions of years. Researchers are offering their proofs in support of these models (evolution and Intelligent Design), but there seems to be a common point between the two: neither model can be conclusively proved in a laboratory, and at the end both are accepted based on a personal conviction. I choose to believe in the biblical world view, and I do not want to adjudicate between the different world views here. However, I want to point out that the theory of evolution has had a profound effect on how we think about marriage, because evolution affects our thinking whether we believe it or not.

In the age of Creationism humans viewed themselves as being in the image of the Creator. This idea gave humans dignity and they rated themselves higher than other creatures, having an added responsibility to take care of and protect the rest of creation, and to become more like the One whose image they bore. All the reference points of human life pointed upwards, so humans were supposed to measure their deeds in the light of God's principles and to judge all good or evil based on this. Evolution turned this reference system upside down. If humans evolved from lower life forms then those forms had to become the reference points. In this case humans can do whatever their 'ancestors' could, and, furthermore, human behaviour is governed by the same triggers as animal behaviour. From this point it is easy to arrive at the question a reporter once asked me: 'It is proven in nature that monogamy is not a natural or self-evident behaviour. Animals – even hominoid ones – are mating with multiple partners and are not loyal to just one. Shouldn't we, therefore, let go of the idea of monogamous and idealistic marriage and look for other forms of partnership that are more in line with our nature and evolutionary heritage?' While I was thinking of my answer, I suddenly remembered the African lovebird (*Agapornis roseicollis*). These rosy-faced birds are much-loved pets in Europe as well. They choose a mate for life, and are faithful to the end. If one of them happens to die, the other will not choose another mate but often dies as well. This special behaviour earned them their name: lovebirds. Besides these tiny parrots there are other species that are also monogamous. How does this apply to human partnerships? The moral is that we shouldn't compare our behaviour to that of animals. Humans are on a higher level due to our ability to make decisions, to base these decisions on moral and ethical principles, and to feel remorse after mistakes, at least after the first couple of occasions. Humans should be humans and animals should be animals. If I want to frankly answer the reporter's question: there are animals that appear to be human in their behaviour, but it seems there are humans who behave like animals.

Another major effect of evolutionary ideology on marriage is the overemphasis on instincts. This also had a major effect on Freudian psychology. The young Sigmund Freud was amazed by Carl Brühl's lectures about Darwinism at the University of Vienna. Later he used these ideas in his own theory of psychology. According to Freud the instinctual drives formulate the so-called 'id' of the personality, which constantly bombards the higher levels of personality: the 'ego' and the 'superego'. According to Freud, these drives are mostly organised around sexuality, so we are constantly under the pressure to reproduce and to leave our genetic print behind. By accepting this logic we also accept that we are fully under the influence of our sexual drives. Many times my clients say very typical sentences in support of this notion: 'I couldn't do anything: the attraction was so irresistible, I simply gravitated into her/his bed.' 'The amount of sex my wife can provide is simply not enough for me, so I cannot do anything else but supplement it elsewhere.' The most dangerous element in this idea is that it removes individual responsibility and puts the blame on instincts, making way for every kind of uncontrolled deed. In this view of things there are no mistakes, no bad acts, and no sins.

There is one more effect to mention that is also a child of evolution. It is the inequality of humans. Darwin himself put the Caucasian, white-skinned humans at the top of his evolutionary tree and the so-called coloured ones lower down ('negroes' is the term he used), likening Australian Aboriginals to gorillas at the lowest level of humanity. If life is a really big chain of survival where only the strongest survive through natural selection, then humans cannot be equal. This is the reasoning Hitler used to identify the Aryan race as 'superior', and it doesn't matter whether we admit it or not, but this still influences the thinking of many today. This is why two authors are on record as arguing for after-birth abortion in a scientific article that appeared in a medical journal. Yes, you read it correctly: they argued for killing newborn babies based on the logic that humans are not all equal and that newborn babies are not fully developed humans, only potential humans, so they do not have the same human rights (like the right for life).[2] The authors considered only those fully developed humans who can at least minimally contribute to the sustenance of their lives as having all the rights. A baby in need of constant care obviously – in their opinion – doesn't satisfy the criteria. I am the father of two wonderful children, so I will spare you a description of my emotions and thoughts on reading this article. The logic of the article is as curious and frightening as what I encountered in my reading of what was applied to the old, the sick and the handicapped in Hitler's Germany. But how does this relate to marriage? If it is OK to deny the equality of humans, then in marriage too the stronger has the right and the power to manipulate the weaker. This ideology provides one of the best hotbeds of family violence. What does creation suggest in contrast to evolution? Every person bears the image of the Creator: thus, all humans are to receive respect and dignified treatment independently of their skin colour, of their age or of any other differentiating factor. If anyone offends someone else, he offends the One in whose image all humans are made.

As I mentioned before, this book is not written to decide the debate about evolution and creation. But let's suppose there is an unmarried person who has to make a choice between two potential partners. One is upward-looking, navigates life by following a moral compass, believes in monogamy, is committed to a loyal relationship and is not subordinate to his or her instincts but controls them with self-discipline and will, believing that all are equal. The other person looks for right behavioural patterns in the animal kingdom, agrees with changing sexual partners as an uncontrollable and unavoidable phenomenon, and is a person who puts herself or himself above others or will easily subordinate herself or himself. I'm sure that many, if faced with this choice, would choose the former one, just as I did.

The sexual revolution

The sexual revolution was the third-biggest influence, and its lasting effect is still felt today in how we think of marriage. It is again important to see the social climate in which this movement started, and what the issue was against which people started to protest by publicly exposing their sexuality and displaying it without shame. This sexual revolution was a reaction to the prudery that characterised society up until the 1960s. The Victorian morality branded sexuality as something bestial, low and shameful. A decent woman was not expected to show any interest in sexuality, and if she experienced sexual pleasure that was a sure sign of moral depravity. She was to reject the sexual advances of her husband, and if intercourse couldn't be avoided then she was supposed to be as unresponsive as a piece of wood, otherwise her husband might expect this the next time as well. The church had also condemned sex as a necessary evil that was good only for conceiving children, but definitely not for pleasure.

Where were these views of sexuality taken from? Not from the Bible, for sure! In the Bible sexuality is pictured as the beautiful and pleasurable gift of the Creator, who intended it not only for procreation, but for pleasure and the celebration of love. The church's perception of sexuality was formed and influenced for almost fifteen hundred years by Augustine, who fell in love with a woman who was below his social status, so his mother wouldn't let him marry her.

Despite this, they had an illegitimate child, and this caused him to suffer serious pangs of conscience and moral tension. On top of this his mother forced him to marry a woman whom he never came to love. Should we be surprised at all that Augustine was so much against sexuality and women in general? But let's return to our topic and the phenomenon of this sexual revolution. In the 1960s the suppressed feelings of decades, if not centuries, exploded into the open. The hippie movement acted as a catalyst for this eruption by emphasising freedom, emotions and experiences. I bet you also know their war slogan: 'Make love, not war!' This all coincided with the availability of contraceptive pills so nothing could hinder or put a brake on sexual adventures and unlimited sexual freedom. The contributions of the sexual revolution are an integral part of the history of the twentieth century: premarital sex became the norm for many; cohabitation and so-called 'trial marriage' became more common; civil marriage became more and more acceptable; and now, in many societies, it is safer to speak of 'partners' than 'spouses', just to avoid embarrassment.

However, let us ask these questions: What did the sexual revolution deprive us of? How does it still influence our idea of marriage? The influence became significant in two areas: sex and sexuality became disconnected from marriage and took on an exaggerated role in relationships.

Let's start with the first one. Before the 1960s marriage and sexuality were closely tied. Yes, there were infidelity and prostitution, but these were not socially acceptable, nor were they considered compatible with marriage. These were banished into society's shadow world, seldom acknowledged publicly and usually treated as secrets. Language has helped preserve this ostracised social status through the use of somewhat pejorative terms such as 'fornication' to describe extramarital sex. These words show how far our cultural roots still draw on our past norms. In the 1960s sex and sexuality became detached from marriage, and extramarital relationships became legal. These new ideas were supported by famous experts like Carl R. Rogers, the father of humanistic psychology. He even wrote a full volume about the subject with the title, *Becoming Partners: Marriage and Its Alternatives* in 1972. The book is based on an interesting starting position that is not without dangers. According to him the traditional cohabiting forms of humanity, marriage and the nuclear family (father, mother, children), have failed, necessitating the search for new models for intimate relationships. In this way, informal partnerships, free love and the hippies and their communes were answers to the crisis of traditional relationship forms. Rogers welcomes this change as a series of experiments towards a new relationship form and a new value system. As far as he was concerned, when a couple want to live according to the expectations of their parents, society or religion, they disturb and damage the delicate and complicated process of creating a natural form of the marriage relationship.[3] In almost every European country books have been published supporting or promoting these ideas. However, at present, we can state with certainty that the experiment to separate marriage and sexual life has not been successful. Infidelity is just as hurtful today as it was in the past, and attempts to maintain intimate relationships with several individuals concurrently are still destructive of the WE identity. The once-celebrated alternative relationship forms have proved to be even more volatile than the much-criticised traditional marriage. For example, when compared to marriage, partnerships are three to five times more prone to break up, physical abuse is three times more common, alcoholism is also higher, and the life expectancy of the partners is three to four years less when compared to that of spouses. After evaluating the last forty years of experimentation the same can be said about marriage lived in sexual exclusivity that has already been said about democracy: marriage as an institution struggles with challenges and hardships, but no one has come up with a better solution yet.

The other big influence of the sexual revolution on marriage was that it made society believe that no one could or should live without sex. Sex became overvalued and is present everywhere, and here are some examples. When we analyse many advertisements aired on TV during the commercial breaks, we notice that in many cases the goods and services are advertised with some kind of sexually charged or erotic innuendo, either visual or verbal. Sexuality is explicitly or implicitly present in the lyrics of songs, either heterosexual[4] or homosexual[5] in nature. You find sexuality everywhere: in films, in magazines, in radio and on the streets. The message is very obvious: a normal and healthy person is sexually active independently of marital status, age or any other factor. The message is that sex should be part of everyday life, no matter what.

Let me illustrate how deep-seated this notion is with a conversation I had with a single women in her thirties. According to her, most of her relationships broke up because men couldn't keep up with her sexual appetite. What was exciting and joyful for them in the beginning became a high-pressure obligation to maintain. When I asked her what she thought the right time was to start a sexual relationship with her partner, she replied: 'I believe it is not right to start with sex; it is best to get to know each other first.' Then she continued: 'Never on the first date; I usually wait until the second date.'

We then spent two ninety-minute sessions talking about the place and function of sexuality in a relationship, and how important it is to build a foundation for a relationship and to get to know the other person in different situations so they can grow to trust each other. I stressed that this is something that requires time – a long time. At the end of the second session I asked her to summarise what she had learnt and what would she do differently in the future. She said: 'I learnt that I am harming my relationships by letting them become sexual too early. From now on I will wait until we have really got to know each other. I will not hurry, and I have decided to go to bed with a man no earlier than the third date.'

How different that sounds to the following report of a couple about their relationship: 'My husband and I dated for two years before we made love. I know, many find this strange, but it was important for us that it wasn't built on sex. During those two years we got to know each other really deeply; we had time to talk, and to share affection in different ways. When sex happened, it was like trusting my life to him. We never realised then just how important those years would be to us later during our marriage. After the birth of our daughter I had complications and we couldn't be together for months. During that time we had a resource to fall back on, and we started to do the things that we had done while dating. This was really reassuring and it allowed us to feel connected even without sex, while still experiencing each other's love.

Yes, sex is a wonderful experience! It is an important part of the relationship of any loving couple. It is a celebration of their relationship and it deepens their attachment and commitment. It is not true, however, that a relationship can only be good if it is filled with an ever-present sexual charge.

This is a modern myth that stems from the sexual revolution, and we are programmed to believe in it.

Does marriage mean . . . ?
It doesn't matter whether it is consciously or unconsciously, but we are all influenced to some extent by these ideological currents. However, because we put together our own relationship databases from isolated bits of information, together with our own good and bad experiences – mostly unconscious – we end up with a patchwork impression and our conviction is dependent on which ideological current has influenced us the most.

Let us rather develop a common dictionary – a set of terms – that we will all understand. It is also time for me to present you with a definition of marriage that we can use in the rest of the book.

At the moment marriage is defined in many different ways, depending on which country you are living in. Most definitions emphasise mutual attachment and fidelity, and stress the importance of family and emotional security for children. However, I'm sometimes puzzled as to why these definitions mostly tend to give worth to the marriage relationship only if children are involved. In fact, I am left with the feeling that in many countries the laws regard marriage as if it were a useful tool to meet the standards of society, and not something that has an inherent value of its own.

Webster's Encyclopedic Unabridged Dictionary gives the following definition of marriage: 'the social institution under which a man and a woman establish their decision to live as husband and wife by legal commitments, religious ceremonies, etc.' This also leaves me with the feeling that something is missing from this definition. The focus is not on the marriage relationship itself, but more on the act of taking the marriage oath: as if marriage were a matter for a brief moment, and then the couple live happily ever after. This type of thinking is present with couples who are getting ready for the *wedding*, but somehow forget to get ready for what's coming after that: *marriage*.

Professor David H. Olson is one of the most important sources of couples therapy know-how in my praxis (the application of my ideas). He defines marriage the following way: 'the emotional and legal commitment of two people to share emotional and physical intimacy, various tasks, and economical resources'.[6] This definition is based on serious knowledge, and includes the emotional and functional side of the relationship. However, it doesn't seem to fix the present situation or talk much about the planned or hoped-for term of commitment.

Let's examine a definition from ecclesiastical circles: 'a consensual, lifetime union of one man and one woman that is beneficial for the spouses, and is aimed at procreating and raising children'.[7] This text emphasises the long-term aspect of marriage and refers to the consensus of the parties, one of the important criteria upon which its legality is based. However, it makes it look like the ultimate aim of marriage is procreation. If so, what about the couples who cannot have children? Are their marriages incomplete? I believe the most important persons in marriage are the husband and wife, and not the children.

You might think that I'm too critical of others without risking criticism of my own definition. You are right! I should write down my definition too. It might not be perfect, but here it is anyway: 'Marriage is the voluntary, monogamous, life-sharing union of one man and one woman, based on equality, mutual love and commitment, protected by law and made with the intention of lifelong commitment'. For me every bit of this sentence has a special importance:

One man and one woman. There are several variations of marriage that have been tried during human history, like one man and several women, one woman and several men, two men and two women, etc. However, when I talk about marriage in this book, I refer always to the relationship of one man and one woman.

Voluntary. There are cultures, even today, where the age for marriage and the future partner are determined by the parents. In other situations the person seems to choose, but his or her choice is not based on love or the desire to share a life with the other one, but, for example, to run away from the parents. I have seen many cases similar to this. However, for me marriage is always a voluntary bond: a choice made by two people who love each other and want to live together in a shared life.

Based on mutual love and commitment. Maybe love is the more obvious of the two criteria, but commitment is equally important. The marriage cannot be built solely on emotions. There are situations when it becomes harder to love the partner, but we still owe fidelity to our spouse. Although it may be hard to feel the love, we remain loyal to our partner because of our promise. And, after all, that promise is not dependent on my partner, but on me. I made the promise. This attitude could prove a great resource at a time when the relationship must be restored: for example, when infidelity happens. But let's talk about that later.

Equal. This is also an important point to stress. I have heard this comment many times in therapeutic sessions: 'If I as the man can do that . . . then she as the wife has to. . . .' This and similar sentences sound the alarm for me. Maybe it is because I share my life with strong women, my wife and my daughter, but I have become more and more sensitive to statements like this. Usually it becomes clear very quickly that there is a false understanding of male and female roles lurking behind such comments. Let's admit that men and women may be different physically, in functions or their relationship roles – i.e. one is better at building the house and the other at furnishing it; one is good at multi-tasking and the other is not – but they are equal in status and dignity. Any other arrangement will fuel abuse, dominance and humiliation, all of which can kill a marriage relationship.

Monogamous. Marriage is an exclusive relationship that belongs only to the spouses. There is an invisible circle around the husband and wife that no one should violate, and that includes the pretty personal assistant, the macho boss and even the parents and the children.

With the intention of lifelong commitment. I'm the kind of therapist who is willing to fight to the end to save a marriage. However, I also live in reality and have to admit that I cannot help to save (and sometimes shouldn't help to save) all marriages – even if this is the hardest thing for me to say. There are extreme life situations where staying together will cause more harm than if the relationship is brought to a close and the former spouses start building separate new lives. But I find it important to stress: marriage is made with the intention to last for a lifetime. To pronounce this has a profound psychological effect. If you can admit this to yourself, then in the heat of an argument you are unlikely to blackmail or threaten your spouse with divorce. This intention must be clear and public at all times.

Protected by law. Marriage is preferable to all other forms of cohabitation because it has a clear beginning – a moment of commitment – when the two persons involved declare in front of witnesses that from that moment on their relationship is legal. This legality comes with rights and responsibilities. If this is only regarded as a formality, then I might agree with those who claim that marriage is nothing more than a piece of paper. However, the formality has an internal content, and if we take this into consideration, marriage has a qualitative edge over its competitors. I remember how good it felt to speak about Dora as 'my wife' during the wedding ceremony. Our status and role in society changed as well at that point, with profound implications for our relationship. Before Dora I had other girlfriends, but at that moment Dora became someone really unique. There is only one like her. It is great to be able to say: 'She is my wife!' or 'He is my husband!'

Life-sharing union. The sense of community that a wife and husband share encompasses every aspect of life: 'from table to bed', as we say. This permeates their leisure time, the choosing of a home, their finances, spirituality and everything else. The person who enters into marriage binds his or her life entirely to the other's life. In marriage there is no such thing as sharing a portion of life. This doesn't mean that from now on I cannot have my own hobby or personal friends, but it does mean that from now on I'm first and foremost a husband, and only secondarily an angler, a racing enthusiast or a weekend sportsman; I'm first of all her husband, and only secondarily a mate to my friends. This expression also means that couples will share time and space together. A relationship where one partner lives and works far away for extended periods of time, and is seldom at home, is in danger.

Summary

Marriage is the voluntary, monogamous, life-sharing union of one man and one woman, based on equality, mutual love and commitment, protected by law and made with the intention of lifelong commitment.

What this all means for the three types of marriages I presented you with in the beginning of chapter 2 is summarised in the following table.

The three types of marriage and the definition of marriage

Superficial	Functional	Deep
The partners didn't formulate a concept of what they mean to each other. They do not share the same definition of marriage.	The couple live in a well-defined relationship and know who they are to each other. However, they do not have an agreement as to what the most important values of their relationship are; neither have they defined what is acceptable in the relationship and what constitutes a violation of its borders.	The couple know exactly who they are to each other, and live in a legal relationship. The formal frame of the relationship is filled with true content. They have talked about the values of their relationship and agreed on the rules. They are aware of the behaviour that will contribute to their relationship and of that which would damage the mutual trust.

Exercises

Answering the questions below will help you to make use of the principles presented in this chapter in your own relationship, and to practise them in everyday life. Answer these questions honestly! If you wouldn't like your partner to see them, use a separate sheet that you can dispose of later. It is important that you do not contemplate your answer for long, but that you write it down as soon as possible. The words will have a real effect only if they are pronounced or written down!

1. Who is your partner for you?
2. Who do you think you are in this relationship?
3. Can you list typical sentences or keywords that suggest that your relationship is based on a mutually recognised contract?
4. What does this contract say about:
   - fidelity?
   - money?
   - standing by each other?
   - your relationship with your children?
   - your relationship with the parents?
   - your roles in the relationship?
   - any other important issues?
5. To what extent does your relationship meet the definition of marriage given above?
   - voluntary:
   - monogamous:
   - life-sharing union:
   - of one man and one woman:
   - based on equality:
   - based on mutual love and commitment:
   - protected by law:
   - made with the intention of lifelong commitment:
6. What would you change in your relationship in order for it to work better?

[1]Skrabski Árpád & Kopp Mária, *A boldogságkeresés útjai és útvesztői a párkapcsolatokban* (Budapest: Szent István Társulat, 2010), p. 74. [2]Alberto Biublini & Fransesca Minerva,

'After-birth abortion: why should the baby live?' *Journal of Medical Ethics*, 2013/39/5, pp. 261-263. [3]I'm paraphrasing his opinion from Carl. R. Rogers, *Partnerschule: Zusammenleben will gelernt sein - das offene Gespräch mit Paaren und Ehepaaren*, pp. 196-197. [4]There are plenty to choose from; just to mention some iconic songs: *Let's make a night to remember* by Bryan Adams; *All I wanna do is make love to you* by Heart; or *I drove all night* by Celine Dion. [5]*I kissed a girl* by Katy Perry or *Let's go outside* by George Michael [6]Olson & DeFrain, *Marriage & Families: Intimacy*, p. 3. [7]*Catholic Lexicon;* source: *http://lexikon.katolikus.hu/H/Házasság.html* (date: 2/9/2014).

Define and guard the borders of your relationship

4

If I had to single out one principle as the most important, I would choose this one. It determines how many tools we will have to protect our marriage against intruders. Infidelity doesn't start when a stranger steps into the inner circle of the relationship. It starts when we leave a gap in the wall that shields our relationship. If there is a gap, sooner or later someone is going to step inside.

I promised earlier that I would open up personally. As I progress into the subject of infidelity, I feel this book might be one of the most important books I have ever written. I find this topic so important that I am willing to become vulnerable by disclosing parts of my personal life story. I trust that you will handle it appropriately. Here come three chapters of my life.

Chapter one of my life

I got married. I was lucky to find the 'real one' while I was very young. We were both 18 years old when we started to date, and after three years we said 'I do'. (I wouldn't suggest to my children that they get married this young, though, even if I have never regretted it.) Long before our wedding day, we had registered to attend a youth camp that was eventually held two months after our wedding. When we arrived at the venue, we were told that they had no room for married couples and that we would have to move into separate quarters with other single participants. Being a pragmatist, I agreed to this, thinking nothing wrong could happen if we had to spend two nights apart. However, Dora squeezed my hand, signalling that I had just done something wrong. I had been too quick to accept the situation and didn't fight for our relationship and ask others to respect its boundaries – just two months after the wedding! I felt I had to make amends for this and tried to demonstrate in every possible way that we are one team. This not only gained some extra points from my wife, but also taught me a life lesson: any time I can intentionally do things that will build a sense of security in our relationship and strengthen our protection against external forces, I should do them, even if these forces aren't sexual in nature.

Another chapter of my life

In the course of time I trained as a clergyman and entered full-time ministry. While I was still at the seminary one of my teachers told me this: 'Be ready for that day when a woman will sit in your office and try to start an affair with you. What will happen will not be decided in that moment, but will have been already decided by what has gone before.' I didn't know what to do with this statement. For me being a minister and having an affair were extreme opposites, very far removed from each other. Today, after two decades of working as a pastor, I know what my professor was referring to. It is my official duty to be kind and understanding, and it can easily happen that some women will experience more kindness during a counselling session with me than they have ever received from their fathers or husbands. This can result in an emotional attachment. What can I do in order not to cross – or to let others cross – my boundaries? I must always remember that I am the leader and the professional in this setting: it is my responsibility to protect both my boundaries and those of my client. I must do everything to prevent infidelity, even in our minds. To this end I set up some rules:

- I intentionally avoid being alone with a woman in the building. If there is someone else around, their presence injects restraint into the situation and also gives my client a sense of security.
- I avoid situations where I would need to travel alone with a woman in my car.
- When I meet or greet a woman I avoid physical contact, and will not hug or kiss even if I see that she intends to. I stretch out my hand and offer a handshake from an appropriate distance. This way I regulate the spatial relationship. Naturally, if there is an older lady, with whom I'm more in the relationship category of mother-son or grandma-grandson, then I do not mind them getting closer physically. It is the same with women who are close friends with both Dora and me.
- Avoiding physical contact is also important in situations where I have to comfort someone. When I console a man it is natural that at the appropriate moment I place my hand on his shoulders, but when I'm in the same situation with a woman I will avoid this, relying solely on verbal communication to express comfort.
- It is also important for me to make it clear to everyone that I live in a happy marriage with Dora. In my local church we hold hands, and express our love towards each other in appropriate ways. This transmits the message,

more than anything else, that there is no place for a third person in our relationship.

Do you feel that I'm exaggerating a bit? Maybe . . . but I must tell you that one of the most painful things for me to see is the life and marriage of a pastoral colleague shattered because he didn't protect his boundaries well enough. I do not wish such a traumatic experience on anyone, which is why I'm advocating prevention so strongly.

A third chapter of my life

I later became a family and couples therapist. This role has many similarities to that of a minister, and the borders have to be protected as well: for example, when the husband cannot be involved in the therapy and the wife comes alone. In such a setting I deploy the same rules as I do as a minister of the church. On top of that there is one more boundary to protect in this setting, and this is the professional relationship with colleagues. A helping professional carries many secrets and burdens as part of the profession, and can become vulnerable in a stressed life situation. Who would be better able to understand these problems than another professional experiencing the same in her own life? Whether it be among teachers, medical doctors, psychologists or couples therapists, it easily happens that they find comfort in the arms of a colleague, which can turn quickly into intimacy.

It is natural that a colleague working in the same area would understand better than the spouse who happens to be an engineer or an economist. This can start emotions and thoughts that can lead to emotional attachment and sexual desires that endanger the marriage relationship. In my opinion, professional conferences and training events where the participants sleep over are especially dangerous places. Also, there are many times that therapists work in pairs in order to represent both sexes in a balanced manner, and the usual team consists of a man and a woman. They will work together, discussing the relationship, the family's problems and their clients' sexual dysfunction, and they can easily build up more than just a professional relationship. I usually work alone, but every time I work in a team I ask my wife to tell me how she feels about it. I want to know her emotions and thoughts about me talking with another woman about the intimate problems of others, and how dangerous she feels this is for our relationship. Does this diminish her trust in me? How would she react if a therapy session were to be protracted, causing me to arrive home late? These are questions that need to be addressed in an honest relationship. It is also important to me that my colleagues know my wife personally, just as I want to know the husbands of these colleagues. Even if these friendships are only superficial, and we rarely meet, this process will help them to have a virtual presence at every therapy session evaluation when I'm alone with the colleague. By asking how the other's spouse is doing, we are making them part of the session and the discussion; they become our virtual witnesses.

The dilemma of the broken radar
You might remember the quotation from Professor Maria Kopp and Árpád Skrabski that says that the marriage ceremony is the end of the search phase. We also saw that this is not an automatic switch connected to the wedding day, but rather an internal process. I have great sympathy and understanding for the way in which a family friend - a very pretty and sweet lady who intentionally guards her

boundaries – talked about this. Once, a male colleague asked her if she knew what a good-looking woman she was. She answered: 'I know exactly how beautiful I am, but I'm exclusively reserving my being-a-beautiful-woman for my husband!'

Too many people live on after their wedding day without narrowing the focus of their 'radar' beams on their spouse alone – without removing the condom from the wallet. They live dangerously, potentially at risk that they will end up in the bed of someone else: and, unfortunately, there are some who are even looking for the possibility. This 'open gate' behaviour can be tracked in several behavioural forms. Let me list some of them.

Double meaning (innuendo)

I once witnessed this interesting conversation while visiting a man who was working in his garden as I arrived. Standing by his beautifully shaped bushes we started to talk. A few minutes later a woman, his neighbour, came over with a plate of tasty-looking cakes. She kindly offered them to us and I gladly accepted, but my friend said that his hands were dirty and that he didn't want to touch them. The woman replied with a cheeky smile: 'OK, I understand, you do not like dirty touchings!' Nothing happened, but the words carried an erotic overtone that lingered for a while. He meant that he didn't want to touch the food, but she was suggestive, implying that he didn't like to sexually stroke others. The woman could have reacted both ways, but she chose to move the discussion into sexually charged territory. This could have been interpreted as an offer.

I have observed how a distant acquaintance likes to use ambiguous comments with women. Somehow all his comments seem to have double meanings and can be interpreted as sexually suggestive signals. By using this technique he was assessing his chatting partners to see if they were open to a fling. He did it in a very clever way, leaving his comments to be interpreted by his listeners in more than one way: so, in case someone told him off, he could answer that the naughty one was the one who thought of naughty things, because he had never intended anything sexual. Dora and I concluded that, sooner or later, he would find someone willing to take the bait, and that he would exploit that option. It didn't take two months before we heard that he was caught up in an affair, and that this wasn't the first time in his marriage.

Testing touches
There are people, men and women alike, who like to intimately touch the person they are speaking to. Some do it in a very explicit way, while others do it more discreetly, like holding a handshake longer than usual. Some like to pick the small bits and pieces off the clothing of the other person and touch them in places that are not socially appropriate. Some like to touch the face, arm or shoulder. At first these touches may feel random, unintentional or even natural. However, if the person is receptive then they become very intentional and more intimate.

It is interesting to observe this in real-life situations. I observed a man during an event, someone whose wife had shared her suspicion with me that he might be involved in an extramarital relationship. A woman was the speaker and the technicians put a microphone on her, but for some reason it wasn't functioning. The man jumped up, ran to her and wanted to be very helpful by checking if the micro port was turned on. In doing this he pulled her blouse up at the back, and in the process of checking the device he grabbed the micro port and managed to touch her back several times. You could see that she wasn't comfortable with the situation, but she didn't protest – although she might have if she could have seen the lustful expression on the man's face, as I could!

Using dating sites and applications

It is a more obvious and more drastic way to violate the boundaries when someone starts to use dating applications with the intention of flirting. Online anonymity and impersonal communication are a big temptation for many, especially if they are trying to get feedback on how much they are worth in the dating 'market'.

A few years ago I was asked to present a talk about the advantages and disadvantages of online dating to singles. During the preparation for it I studied many sites and services and read many adverts in order to help the participants prepare an authentic and effective advert and avoid swindlers. It was just here where I had a few unwanted surprises. For example, I found that a friend's husband had placed an advert without mentioning that he was married with three children! On another site I found someone I used to meet in church gatherings. According to his advertisement a man in his fifties was looking for ladies between 35 and 45 who were interested in accompanying him on a wellness weekend. Because it concerns me when religious people behave so unethically, I decided to ask him what his goal was with this advertising. He told me off, and pointed out that if I had read the text carefully and I hadn't been so judgemental, I would have realised that he wasn't looking for one woman but for several – to be sales representatives for his new business so he could test them at the wellness centre. Our conversation came to an abrupt end, but I had a bad feeling that this business sounded phoney and that the future held some surprises. And it did. A few weeks later, while parking at a shopping mall, I saw the man in a very intimate conversation with a woman other than his wife. He didn't see me, and I was so curious that I decided to wait and see – and, I have to admit, also to prove myself right. It didn't take three minutes and the pair were engaged in a passionate embrace and intimate kissing session. Then the woman got out of the car and the man drove off.

I'm not sharing these stories because they are such choice memories or because I needed to get rid of my frustration. I want to prove an important point: based on the behaviour of a person, it can be stated to a great degree of certainty whether they will end up in an extramarital affair or not. I want us to take this very seriously: your behaviour and that of your spouse – how you relate to each other – will sooner or later make it obvious if you have locked your radar on to your marriage partner, or if you are still searching for someone else.

Inner and outer boundaries
If you got the impression a) that marriages need to be guarded against external, evil forces that want to destroy them; or if you got the impression that b) there are those terrible predators out there who have become upset with their own marriages and are unscrupulously looking for an affair – then it is time for me to add some more detail and information into the story. I do not believe that there is a 'cheater type' that needs to be avoided, or that there is a 'faithful type' that is genetically coded not to commit infidelity. Nobody has a certificate stating that he is unable to cheat. I believe there is a persona in everyone that is

capable of doing deeds we never imagined, once this persona is fed and strengthened and becomes dominant. I rejected this idea for a long time, but then an old professor from Germany changed my mind. He once started his presentation about postmodern philosophy by greeting us with a salute I will never forget: 'I welcome the class of potential murderers!' After waiting for the shock to appear on our faces, he continued explaining: 'Imagine that you are woken up by a loud noise one night. As you come to your senses you realise that there is someone in the house. You silently start searching for the source of the noise. As you approach the room of your five-year-old daughter, you see a strange man lurking around her bed. Now, suddenly a handgun appears in your hand. . . . Could the person who is not going to shoot raise their hand?'

Nobody lifted a hand.

That moment I realised, along with my classmates, that there is a potential killer in me. Later, the teacher explained that through his story he wanted us to see ourselves in a different light. He succeeded.

If I quickly analyse the long list of all the people whom I have helped to come to terms with his or her infidelity, then I have to say that a potential cheater lies dormant in every one of us. It would be good if this persona were never allowed to dominate our thoughts, feelings and actions. By protecting our boundaries we can help keep this persona dormant.

An excerpt from a novel called *The Nightmare*, by Hungarian classical writer Mihály Babits, provides a fitting illustration of this. In the story a rich young gentleman goes to see a prostitute for the first time, and the experience makes him aware of a part of his personality that he hadn't known before.

'I found disgusting the methods I tried to force my arousal. The whole room was so rigid with bare walls, the low washstand, the bed, the night table with the glimmering light: everything emphasised a quick and businesslike usage. I felt myself so removed from all that was familiar to me, from anything that was beautiful, loved and desired, that I started to wonder how I got there and was it really me in that room? Just like an aristocrat finding himself in the dirt. The whole setting didn't radiate erotic beauty as I had imagined; it was rather comical and disgusting.

'However, I forced myself and turned towards the woman and pushed my face into her hair. The smell of a strong perfume surprised my nose and it felt somehow very familiar, and I started to see everything differently. Suddenly I felt a crazy, wild desire and couldn't see anything from the surroundings. I didn't think any more of beauty or of ugliness; I didn't see and didn't feel anything else: only the naked body, the woman's meat beside me and under me. Suddenly, as if transformed, I was nothing more than a mating animal driven by lust.

'And I can say, almost with certainty, that suddenly I woke up for a moment – woke up to my other existence. Yes, I woke up, at least in the morning, early morning, and there was snoring coming from other beds around, and I with an animal satisfaction stretched my limbs on the tainted bed. But this was only for a minute, because after a minute there I was again, Elemér Tábory, the handsome, kind gentleman.

'You can come again some other time to see me,' said the girl as we stood outside the door, and (she looked a very sentimental young girl) she wanted to kiss my cheek. But I couldn't help myself and turned away, but, suddenly realising how bad it must feel to her, I kissed her myself at the end.

'I never felt myself so disgusted as then, on that morning walking home, knowing that there is someone else living in me: a brutal, harsh, dirty, selfish and unhappy creature that I hate, but who is also me.'[1]

For sure, until faced with a real-life situation, no one can say what variations of his or her personality live within. Maybe, if we knew this person, we would be horrified the same way as Elemér Tábory was. Thus, the boundaries protect us not only from third-party intruders, but also from our dark side, which is awakened by a chance situation or an unexpected opportunity. We must protect our boundaries from attacks from the outside – and from the inside as well!

Not just survival

As I mentioned before, infidelity is a long process in which sexual infidelity happens only at a late stage. Up until the first coitus a long row of boundaries (sometimes even 20 or more) are violated, and many inner boundaries that we set for ourselves. The following story illustrates this process.

The Smiths had been living together for ten years. Mr Smith was working for a courier service; his wife was a nurse in a nursing home. Their marriage was very average. Mrs Smith worked a lot, barely spending time at home. Mr Smith worked flexible hours and had free time even during the day. Mrs Smith decided to submit her application to become the head nurse of the nursing home, but she didn't have the self-confidence to share her plans with her husband. 'He wouldn't understand; he is only thinking of how to make more money, and how I could make more money,' was how she justified her decision.

Mr Smith had a hunch that his wife was not being totally honest with him, but he believed that she was overworked and that he had to share her attention. He was wondering whether he should share with her his idea of starting a private business: after all, he had got to know the courier service well enough not to have to work for others. He felt that she could support him while he launched his venture, but still decided not to speak to her about his dream.

It so happened that one day he popped into a coffee shop for a quick snack. As he was leaving he noticed a woman standing behind him in the queue who had long hair and green eyes. As their eyes met she flashed him a smile. In the evening, as Mrs Smith was filling in her application, his thoughts wandered to the woman from the coffee shop. 'There is nothing wrong in noticing other women as well; it won't do any harm,' he convinced himself. The next day he dropped into the same shop, not even admitting to himself he was hoping to meet the woman again. He was lucky on the third day, and as they were standing in the queue Mr Smith started a casual conversation: 'Are you on your lunch break?'

'Yes; this shop is the closest,' she answered. They introduced themselves, sat at the same table, and soon became regular lunch partners. 'There is nothing wrong in eating lunch with a woman, anyway,' thought Mr Smith. Vera, the green-eyed woman, was working for a nearby accounting company and was very smiley and kind – and divorced. The lunch break conversations started to have an effect on Mr Smith's thoughts. In the evenings, as he talked to his wife, or when she turned down his approaches, he tended to think of what Vera would do. What was she doing at the moment? What kind of woman was she? In the mornings, as he was getting ready, he spent more time improving his looks. He shaved better; he used some toothpaste and even some cologne. It started to feel as if he were a teenager again, preparing for a date.

And it happened. One evening when Mrs Smith was working late, which was usually the case, Mr Smith invited Vera out for dinner and a chat - they had already shared phone numbers. Naturally, he said nothing about this to his wife: she would not have understood him anyway. She would have become hysterical and would have supposed that there was something between them. Vera accepted the invitation and a few hours later they were in an embrace. As he reflected on things later, he just couldn't remember how it all happened.

So, how did it happen? How did casual eye contact and a quick smile transform into a sexual relationship? As you can see, in the history of the Smiths their relationship had already started to deteriorate long before there was any sign of Vera, the 'evil intruder'. The couple should have been honest about their feelings and dreams, and found the time to communicate them to each other. However, they not only closed the communication window; they even built a wall between them. The husband was not willing to share his ideas about a possible private business venture and the wife was not sharing her career dreams and insecurities. As trust deteriorated in their relationship, secrets arose. The wall they built was capable of shielding the new, budding relationship of the husband that was not really a relationship - or was it? As he felt that his marriage was getting worse, he was less likely to feel bad about violating its boundaries. The more he got to like Vera, and the stronger the feelings he developed, the more negatively he started to view his marriage and his wife. Then he started to compare his wife to Vera, and she lost out to the witty, kind, clever, pretty and sexy accountant. And then came the most dangerous twist of the story: Mr Smith fell in love while he was still married to Mrs Smith, and he knew this was not right. This tension, or, as therapists call it, cognitive dissonance, could not be maintained in the long run, so his mind started to fabricate excuses that would dissolve his guilt and let him continue on the road of infidelity. The easiest way to achieve this was by putting down his wife in his internal dialogue and re-evaluating the framework of his marriage. Through this process Mr Smith is able to reinterpret his wife's interest in him as her being controlling; her desire for a clean and well-ordered home as obsessive compulsiveness; and her need for closeness as stifling. This ends in a paradoxical situation where the cheater will lose his trust in the one who is being cheated, and start to feel loyal towards the lover whom he trusts (more than he should, actually).

As we went through this extended process, we could see that – before any external sexual links were created – the internal emotional attachment between the spouses was lost, which made their relationship vulnerable to external intruders. The task that this sets us is twofold: on the one hand the boundaries of the relationship must be guarded, and on the other hand there should be constant work to improve the relationship in order to build a vibrant, joyful marriage that represents a value worth protecting and for which it is fine to make sacrifices.

Summary

Based on the behaviour of a person, it can be stated to a great degree of certainty whether the person will ever end up in an extramarital affair or not. To guard the boundaries means that we must actively avoid double meaning (innuendo) in our communication, physical touch of the other sex, and even the more innocent versions of virtual dating. It is also important to examine the situations that arise in our work/study/leisure activities in order to take appropriate steps to prevent violating the boundaries of our relationship.

What this all means for the three types of marriage I presented to you in the beginning of chapter 2 is summarised in the following table.

The three types of marriage and guarding the boundaries

Superficial	Functional	Deep
The couple are not intentional in guarding their borders; the gates are partially open. Sometimes they are looking for an adventure or they simply cause dangerous situations themselves. Situations prone to misinterpretation or boundary violations can often happen.	The partners are committed and they are not looking for extramarital adventures, but are not aware of the importance of the boundaries. They aspire to a good relationship but accidents can happen which leave much guilt in their wake.	The couple are aware of the importance of the boundaries. Because they have stopped the searching phase, they aim to eliminate all dangerous or dubious situations. They have made conscious decisions as to how they will defend their boundaries in different situations. They are committed to defend these boundaries and to enrich their relationship.

Exercises

Answering the questions below will help you to make use of the principles presented in this chapter in your own relationship and practise them in everyday life. Answer these questions honestly! If you wouldn't like your partner to see them, use a separate sheet that you can even throw away. It is important that you do not contemplate your answers for long but write them down as soon as possible. The words will have a real effect only if they are pronounced or written down!

1. At the beginning of the chapter, I wrote down what steps I take to guard the boundaries of my relationship. Now it is your turn to write down your rules in the different areas of your life.
   - The boundaries in my work:
   - The boundaries in my leisure activities:
   - The boundaries in my friendships:
   - The boundaries in other areas:
2. What type of boundaries would you expect your partner to draw?
   - The boundaries in his/her work:
   - The boundaries in his/her leisure activities:
   - The boundaries in his/her friendships:
   - The boundaries in other areas:

If you have a chance, share the thoughts and emotions that came up while you were working on this exercise.

3. What type of boundary violations could be specially dangerous in your marriage?
   - Threats in your behaviour:
   - Threats in your partner's behaviour:
4. Besides guarding your boundaries, it is also important to work on your relationship and strengthen it. We will deal in more detail with this topic later, but I want you to write up some ideas that will contribute to the growth in your relationship.

[1] Mihály Babits, *The Nightmare*, chapter 5.

5 Don't put the past aside, but put it right

A few years ago I drove to a funeral with a retired pastor. On the road we were talking about old times and new challenges. Among other issues, we talked about a young couple who were on the brink of divorce. We tried to make sense of what was happening to them, and I happened to say something like this: 'I can understand them; it is not easy with the baggage that they have. Both of them grew up in broken families and suffered much trauma in their childhood.'

Uncle Joe's reply made me really think about the whole issue. 'Gábor, do not play the psychologist with me. I know very well what a hard childhood means, but I have been faithful to my wife for more than fifty years!' I asked him to tell me about his childhood, and his life story turned out to be like something straight from a Mark Twain novel. 'I was born before the war. Because my father had a German name, he was called up to serve in the German army. When my mother was left alone, she didn't know what to do with me. She gave me up to a foundling hospital. This is how I learned to survive very early on. When I was big enough I was sent to live with foster parents. This meant something very different in those days: we were basically cheap labour. At the age of nine I had to plough the fields and my master got two sets of clothing and some money to keep me. I was supposed to get half a loaf of bread and 100 grams of bacon a day, but I tell you, there were more days when I got nothing than days when I got anything. I ate whatever was edible around me. In the summer I watched the cows. I figured that what they could eat, I could eat too. In the winters I ate soaked wheat and corn that I stole from the stables. I even ate fodder and pumpkin reserved for animals. When my master wasn't looking, I even milked the cows straight into my mouth.

'When I couldn't bear it any longer, I escaped, but that didn't make my situation any better, because the gendarmes caught me, beat me and returned me to my master to be beaten again. It happened every day; he would even beat me with a whip or a wooden log. I even lost my consciousness at times. I went into hiding many times to cry, and wished, "If only I had a mother too. . . ." When I turned twelve I was placed elsewhere, where I could eat at the table (for the very first time in my life), attend school, and work only after classes. They were so kind to me; they planned to adopt me, but my mother turned up and took me home with her. As it turned out, she had just had a second child and needed some help with childcare. The little one was the favourite.

'After two years, when I was fourteen, I went to study and started as an apprentice. First thing in the morning, before school, I went to do the daily shopping for a grocer. I earned 200 forints with that work, along with a daily sandwich with either cheese or sausage. In the afternoons I hung around the sugar factory, and tried to help with whatever they'd let me. After half a year I was working so much that I received one kilo of candy every day, plus the 400 forints a month the workers collected for me among themselves. In the evenings

I went to the wood factory, where I dipped chess figures into paint in return for a sack of wood. I brought everything home to support the family, and my mother was so thankful that she gave me the skin of the sausage and let my little brother eat the sausage.

Later on, I finished school with distinction and became a 'brazier'. I received 34 forints as a stipendium each month, but for shovelling a hundred kilos of coal at the train station I received an extra 38 forints. I learned even more skills at the railway factory. I started to work for the railways and earned good money. I went to a village called Magyarcsanád to demolish a bridge. I was nineteen at that time, and I got to know my wife there. I used to joke that I worked in such deep mud at Magyarcsanád that I got stuck there for the next twenty-five years. Then I was drafted into the army. After the army I went on to study, and I became a fire inspector, then a labour inspector. Then I received an invitation to become a pastor. This wasn't an easy decision, as I had also been asked to be the mayor. I decided to study theology; I pastored several congregations and built nine churches altogether all over the country. As you can imagine, we had difficult times, but I could always discuss things with my wife, and that meant a lot to me.

'Yes, my past did leave its imprints on me, but today I can even laugh about the twists and turns my life has taken. And, above all, I'm very thankful that God was with me and helped me through. You know, even the ugliest things can become more beautiful as time passes.'

When I asked him if I could write his story into my book, he told me: 'Gabor, you have to write it down in a way that people will learn to make decisions and not to hide behind their past!'

This chapter is exactly about that! If we do not face our

past, then we condemn ourselves to repeat it over and over again. I invite you, therefore, on a somewhat painful but very beneficial journey. In this chapter I would like to help you to deal with your past and identify factors that threaten your present life and marriage. Do not worry: I will not leave you alone with threatening thoughts, but I will assist you with some handrails that will help you, and give you some tools to assess where you are in the process. The first important fact that I would like you to remember is this: we do not owe our future to our past. We owe it to ourselves to process the past so we can be free to live the future. The past is no excuse for any present bad behaviour, but it is a challenge to change for the better.

A cupboard filled with skeletons
I rarely go to see a doctor, but when I do I'm always surprised by how much people enjoy their problems. While listening to the conversations in the waiting room I sometimes find it hilarious how the patients try to outdo each other with their illnesses. It is almost as if they are vying for a 'Worst Condition' award!

It is interesting, however, that no matter how open and transparent people may be about their physical problems, they go into extreme denial when it comes to their emotional problems, even if these can have a more negative effect on their everyday life than the physical ones. The past impacts that influence our marriage can be grouped into three different categories. There are injuries that we received in our family of origin. Then there are injuries that we collected in our previous relationships that we carry on into our new ones. In the third group are the injuries that stem out of traumatic events unrelated to our family or relationships (for example, accidents, serious illness, the death of a partner, sexual abuse by a stranger). These are very random events and cannot be put into any of the previous categories. No one can get ready for them either, and prevention is not an option, so I cannot deal with them in this book – they deserve a separate volume.

The injuries from your family of origin

It might be expected that the family of origin will have a profound effect in adult life. And because of this many of us do not give it the attention it deserves, even though our past is with us all the time. Sometimes it feels just like a terrible weight pinning us to the ground. On the other hand, if we are parenting right now, this means we are forming a family of origin for our children that is going to serve as their own point of orientation, and provide them with relationship patterns that will make their adult life easier or harder.

The role of the family of origin cannot be over-emphasised. Imagine the years spent with our parents and siblings as the programming period. When we grow up, and become conscientious enough, we are then able to take charge of our life through deliberate decisions. However, there are situations where we cannot keep our hands on the steering wheel. This can be in a crisis situation or any other situation in which we happen to find ourselves, in which we feel unable to make a conscious decision. Naturally, life doesn't stop at these moments, but we are not consciously leading any more. When we let go of the steering wheel like this, the autopilot starts working, and it is not programmed by us, but by our family of origin. We do not even have access to the programming of the autopilot, as it is made up from the impacts, experiences, patterns, problem-solving methods and slogans that all happened long ago in our family. It can be said that from the characteristics of one's family of origin their behaviour in a given conflict or other problem situation can be predicted. The Couple Checkup that I introduced before contains a Couple and Family Map, which provides personal information on this topic.

It is easy to see that the family of origin has a great influence in shaping how its children will react in future situations. These experiences can be categorised into three subgroups.

1. The right balance of dependence and independence

From an early age our minds are the battlefield of two constant forces. One of them urges us to belong, to attach, to form WE – to identify as part of a family. The other force pushes us in the opposite direction. It wants us to become a unique individual: able to live independently of any group and not be vulnerable to others. It wants each of us to have our own opinions and will, and to make our own decisions. This battle can be observed quite clearly in the lives of small children. They may have a tantrum because they want to pick their clothing for the day, and they will resist their parents' having a say in it (independence). On the other hand, they may beg their parents to stay a little more to hold their hands before falling asleep (attachment). These two forces are at play at all stages of life. If they get out of balance, with one of them becoming dominant for a long time, then our life and personality might get distorted. This is summarised in Figure 1:

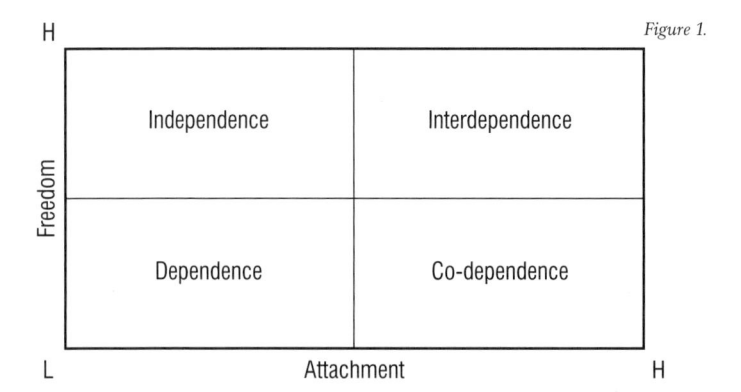

Figure 1.

	Independence	Interdependence
Freedom	Dependence	Co-dependence

Vertical axis: L to H (Freedom). Horizontal axis: L to H (Attachment).

Both forces are very important for a balanced and emotionally healthy life. We have to be able to form attachments as well as draw boundaries. If we are able to balance these opposing forces, then we are capable of forming intimate relationships in adulthood. We are able to connect to a family, to a partner, to the society, while still maintaining self-worth, even in a lonely state. We are able to state our opinion without fear, because we feel secure and are not afraid to lose the support of our peers, even if we are not in agreement. If our ideas are rejected and our will is broken down in childhood, an unbalanced state of fusion results. Families that model this state erase the boundaries of independence. The child feels insecure and indifferent, and needs the presence of the family at all times. The parents tolerate the children only if they show unconditional obedience. There is no place for saying no, and any alternative opinions are interpreted as treason. As grown-ups these children are prone to co-dependence and want to pursue the same type of enmeshed relationship with their partners. The partner is rarely capable of tolerating this emotionally suffocating environment and the relationship ends quickly. Therapy is needed to facilitate change, and a very important goal is to help the person to draw boundaries for the 'I' and learn to protect it. Paul Watzlawick told a story once about a group therapy session where a client had difficulties in saying 'no'. He used the technique of paradox intention by asking the lady to go to every member of the group and say 'no' to whatever they requested.

The lady replied: 'Sorry, I'm unable to do what you are asking for. Ask anything else, but I cannot do this.'

'Very well done! You have already said no to me! Just go on to the next person,' answered Watzlawick.

When the boundaries of 'I' are very well defined but there is no attachment to the other members of the family, separation develops. These children usually get everything financially, but receive little other attention or recognition from their parents. It is very difficult to activate the support resources of the family. For example, nothing will happen if the parents get to know that the child hasn't been to school for two weeks. On the other side, the enmeshed family will have a crisis if the child won't eat their dessert. Upon reaching adulthood, this type of child will find it hard to commit, will demand a great deal of independence, and will see loyalty as a threatening bondage. The person would rather use the partner than love the partner. There is also another possibility when there is no attachment or independence, and it is called chaos. This person is unable to attach and doesn't want to direct their life either. They become lost in their personal relationships and will find it hard to make decisions. Such a person is clearly lost.

As it is often said, the family of origin has to give two things to the child: roots and wings. If both are given and present, intimacy becomes a possibility. If only wings are given without roots, there is alienation. If there are roots, but no wings, there is fusion. If none are present, there is chaos.

2. How does the relationship or the family function?

Where should a child learn how a family functions if not within their own family? Without receiving lessons on family life, the children simply learn by experience. They learn how to communicate emotions. They learn which expressions and methods of communication are acceptable in an emotional matrix, and which are harmful. It is also a very important course in how to resolve conflicts, because conflict resolution can be destructive as well as constructive. During a constructive conflict resolution the tensions are resolved in such a way that the partners are drawn closer to each other. These are the fights after which it feels good to make love. Destructive conflict resolutions are those that end without closure and a real solution, as one party usually ends up forcing their will on the other, which results in alienation and emotional injuries. These are fights after which we do not even want to see each other. The child observes and learns and uses these as their pattern later on in life. So, unless you consciously make efforts, you will pass on the same kind of relationship patterns that you inherited from your parents, and this will go on from generation to generation.

3. Male and female roles

As an integral part of growing up we need to be exposed to a fair amount of both male and female roles in the family. Instability in the family is harmful to this aspect of the process of maturing. Imagine yourself in the place of the children. Steve's parents have divorced and he lives with his mother, who is under financial pressure and must work overtime quite often in order to provide for the family. For this reason, Steve is in a nursery where he is cared for by a woman. After this Steve goes to a playgroup, where again a woman is his primary caregiver. And at last, in primary school, his teachers are also women. The chances are that Steve will finish secondary school without experiencing in a close relationship how males function. Is it surprising then that he cannot act like a man? One client told me that she would be happy to find a reliable man to trust, to rely on and to feel secure with, but in her experience there are only either 'Mr Beans' around, or 'machos', who just want to use her as an object. I need to note that it is not easy for girls to grow up without a male pattern either. For a little girl it is her father who is the first man in whose presence she learns how it feels to be a woman. If the father loves her, values her, hugs her and affirms her from an early age, she learns what it means to be respected and what a genuine man is like. When the time comes and a potential partner treats her the same way, she will identify those familiar patterns and be receptive to his signals. However, if she meets a man who does not show her respect she will sense the contrast – the tension between the pattern she is used to and this man – and won't stay long in the relationship. This explains why women often stay in abusive relationships. In many cases it happens because they have had an abusive father and are pre-programmed to accept that real men are abusive, and that women deserve it and must accept this. It is very difficult to step out of this vicious circle.

When my son was in the glory of his teenage years,

questioning all the values of his parents, I observed how he treated his girlfriend. I was amazed at how similar his behaviour was to mine. The exact same words that I used to court Dora, he was using to court his girlfriend. He held hands with his girlfriend just as it is my custom to hold Dora's hand. Actually, his behaviour was a carbon copy of his parents' relationship, and, at least on the level of appearances, he did what we did. The moral of the story: we might want to be different from our parents; however, when the autopilot kicks in, we start to copy their behaviour and to follow their pattern without thinking, which can have definite pros and cons!

To live in healthy balance with the I and WE depends a great deal on what we call setting up boundaries. The functioning of the family will determine to a great extent whether we will be able to do this in adulthood. A healthy, well-functioning family:[1]

- allows the family members to express their opinions freely;
- accepts disagreements, and, in the case of such differences, no one has to fear rejection;
- encourages family members to think as individuals;
- helps the family members to discover and develop individual skills and talents;
- allows anger to be expressed in an appropriate way;
- sets up boundaries and communicates consequences, but doesn't cause fear or guilt;
- maintains respect for family members even when they disagree;
- allows the children to make age-appropriate decisions.

Contrary to which, in a dysfunctional family:
- The parents invoke shame and guilt in order to curb the

child's effort to gain independence.
- Those who disagree are penalised.
- The parents react with hostility to the anger of the child.
- In the name of solidarity, they place more value on obedience and conformity than on healthy independence.
- The children are in danger of emotional, physical or sexual abuse that can damage their sense of ownership over their bodies and their personhood.
- Children feel responsible for the happiness of their parents.
- The parents 'save' (shield) their children from experiencing the consequences of their actions.
- The parents are inconsistent in their discipline.
- The parents take responsibility for their adult children.

The boundaries are there to help to maintain a good balance of I and WE. Neither of the following situations is good: that parents are emotionally too close to their children; or that they are too removed. Hans Jellouschek lists several cases where this lack of balance can be connected to infidelity. Among those types he mentions the 'daddy's girl' and 'molly-coddle' phenomena. He calls the 'molly-coddled' man the one who continues to live within the enchanting influence of his mother even as an adult. He should have given up the primary place of his mother – the first woman in his life – in order to be available for the love of another woman. Instead he continues to live under the control of his mother, and is therefore not free for another woman due to this internal bondage.[2] He calls the woman who lives within the enchanting influence of her father into adulthood a 'daddy's girl'. Owing to the fact that she is not at peace with her mother, she cannot accept her own womanhood. For this reason, she either tries to overemphasise the 'daddy's girl' role, or she displays masculine qualities.[3]

Based on my own observations I will highlight three more types of unbalanced behaviour that can play a role in someone becoming either a cheater or the victim of infidelity.

- **The child who is used as a surrogate partner.** When the parents get emotionally estranged there is a temptation to gain emotional balance by using the child in a support role. The child is thus forced into an adult role and becomes a 'parent', which is called the process of parentification. These children are very mature for their age; they often carry heavy responsibilities and end up doing a large portion of the household chores. As adults they find it difficult to build emotional relationships based on equality because they are used to a servile and care-giver role. They also learn to put their own needs second, after everyone else's needs. The partner finds this very appealing as it is a very nice feeling to be served, but after a while this behaviour will damage intimacy, resulting in the feeling that they lack a real partner. The 'parentificated' adult will react to this by trying to provide even more care, which will in turn alienate the partner even further.

- **The child growing up in an emotional desert.** I mentioned previously how important it is that parents express their love towards their children. Physical touch, eye contact, quality time together and undivided attention all play pivotal roles in expressing love. The person who hasn't received these as a child can grow up with a very insecure sense of self-worth. I was really shaken by the case of a woman who managed to navigate her marriage to the brink of divorce by repeatedly cheating. She always seemed to end up in an affair with an older man who was kind to her. These men caressed, cuddled and complimented her exactly as a father should treat his daughter. When I asked her about her relationship with her father – how he had expressed his love to her, what her childhood memories were – she started to sob uncontrollably. She tried hard, but she couldn't remember one single occasion when her father had caressed her or said that he loved her. This lack of love from her father left a great void in her heart. It's no wonder that she was vulnerable to the affections of older men who were willing to fill this great emotional need in her heart. You can imagine how these relationships all ended. These men abused the situation and forced her into a sexual relationship, and she sank deeper and deeper into despair. She started to hate herself, struggled with a growing feeling of guilt, had less and less self-worth and moved ever further away from her husband.

- **The abused child.** The most evil of family dysfunctions is when the children suffer emotional, physical or sexual abuse at the hands of those who are supposed to protect them. I will deal further with this topic later, but at this point I want to stress how damaging the effects of abuse are. Instead of seeing themselves as loveable, acceptable and valuable in their own right (to be loved for who they are), such children develop a misconception that they are loveable, acceptable and valuable only if they do certain things (to be loved for doing things). And, because the expected performance is sexual in nature, they quickly learn to feel loveable, acceptable and valuable only if they perform sexually. Without their being aware of it, sexuality becomes a language through which to communicate with the outside world. Subconsciously they will send erotic signals, behave in a sexually provocative manner and flirt – and there will always be someone ready to respond in the same way.

Injuries from the previous relationships

Besides the injuries sustained in the family of origin, many also struggle with injuries inflicted on them in their previous relationships, all of which are heavy burdens for them to bear. In reality, these unprocessed traumas end up determining their next partner of choice. Not long ago a man said this at a therapy session: 'If I think about my partners for the previous ten years, I can see that each new partner was the exact opposite of her predecessor: as if I were trying to compensate.' He couldn't have put it more precisely. Whole therapeutic schools have been built on the unconscious factors involved in choosing a partner. Hans-Joachim Thilo lists the following variations[4] that can cause a relationship to derail:

- **The partner as a substitute.** This constellation develops if someone chooses a person in order to substitute another person, who used to be present in his or her life. The slogan of the relationship is: 'You have to be like him/her!' One of my male acquaintances wanted to date a certain woman, but she refused. Then, once he had got another woman as a partner, he expected her to wear similar clothing to the woman who had turned him down. The relationship didn't last long (fortunately).

- **The partner as an alter ego.** In this type of relationship the partner uses his or her mate to serve his or her narcissism. The person wants to elevate him or herself by becoming the partner's idol. They want the partner to accept their supremacy and to be their loyal follower. The slogan of this relationship is: 'You have to be like me!' However, no partner's aim is to be like the other, and such a relationship is doomed. The other person's destiny is to be him or herself, and to be respected and accepted for who he or she is.

- **The partner as the ideal self.** This is the opposite of the previous setup. One partner idealises the other one, and sees their qualities as being better than they really are. The slogan is: 'You have to be the person I never could become!' This type of relationship will not succeed either, simply because the person will not love the partner for the person they are, but as an idol that they want to be.

- **The partner as a scapegoat.** This is a typical behaviour of passing on responsibility and blame. Those who have never had to bear the consequences of their actions cannot deal with responsibility as an adult because their parents always took it on themselves. For this reason they are looking for a mate who is weak and self-sacrificing, and who will take the blame for all the bad that happens in the home and the relationship. The slogan is: 'Everything is your fault!' If the partner happens to be someone who was abused, the combination becomes explosive.

- **The partner as a buddy.** This type of person needs someone who is close by and can be leaned on: someone with whom they can have an evening out or other leisure activity, but still retain their personal freedom and avoid commitment to the relationship. The slogan of this 'friendship with benefits' is: 'Be available, but do not have expectations!' The end of the relationship usually comes when one partner wants to commit to the next level (shared household, marriage, child, etc.).

Steps of processing

I believe we have diagnosed a fair amount of dysfunction and various relational dead ends. We have got to know some hypotheses about what can go wrong and several possibilities as to what could be the source of a problem. Let us now concentrate on what can be done to overcome a negative trajectory. How can we process the past? I have to stress at the beginning, though, that not every past injury can be processed without the help of an experienced therapist.

I will share some useful techniques; however, I do not want you to concentrate on the methods: rather, try to understand the principles. The following principles can help you a lot – not just to put the past aside, but to put it right.

1. Instead of fleeing, face it!

Fleeing is very dangerous, because in many cases what you flee will simply become more frightening and more powerful. For example, if a person is struggling with acrophobia and avoids bridges, this fear of heights will increase and not decrease. For example, the person who is afraid of bridges will soon be afraid of ladders as well. This is also how the fear pertaining to relationships works. The cause of insecurity, anxiety and distress must be faced. This confrontation can happen in real life (*in vivo*, as the professionals call it), or in the imagination (*in sensu*).

A *real* confrontation can happen in a situation, for example, where someone realises that their parents' behaviour or marriage is influencing their own relationships and sits down with them to talk this through. Sometimes this can end up unleashing a storm, which might actually be the very thing that is needed. Things cannot be undone by acting as if they haven't happened, but if the other side admits the wrongdoing and acknowledges how much pain they have caused to the one they should have protected, it can heal many wounds. I know a person who brought up issues with his parents and caused quite a turmoil. First the parents reacted by rejecting the claims and trying to minimise the problem, but eventually they accepted the blame and realised their mistake. This became a turning point in their relationship. They apologised that they had put a heavy burden on him via their own relationship problems and their emotional rigidity, and started to give to the grandchildren what they had failed to give to the child. The man said that he never thought his parents could develop such a close relationship with his children, and to see his father play football with his son felt like a rewrite of his own childhood. Yes, confrontation and resolution can heal wounds – even retrospectively!

Naturally, confrontations cannot always be had in person (for example, if the parents have died), and sometimes may not achieve their purpose (as in the case of an abusive partner who is no longer around). In these cases there are other options available. In therapeutic sessions I often ask the persons to write a letter to the person with whom the client wants to settle things. It may not be necessary or possible to send such a letter to the intended recipient; however, just to write it feels empowering. Positive changes already start to happen if the person stops fleeing and deals with their emotions, faces certain facts and traumas, and expresses a willingness to let go of the hurt. The most important content surfaces during these moments. Here are some examples:

- 'You cannot imagine how terrible it was when you removed the door of my room when I was fourteen, so that I couldn't close it. That was the only safe place to hide when you were fighting, and you took it away in a split second.'

- 'I was only eight when I found your videotapes and magazines. Throughout my whole teenage years I tried to be different from you. I didn't know if Mum knew about your porn addiction, but I lived in fear, afraid that she would not be able to deal with it and that the family would fall apart.'

- 'The only thing about male-female relationships I learned from you was never to save on flowers. This I've learnt. It would have been good if you could have taught me something more.'

- 'It doesn't matter how hard I try: I cannot remember that you ever let me sit on your lap or let me ride on your neck. I thought this was normal, but then I saw what other daddies did with their little ones. When I heard others call their girls 'sweet' and 'princess', I felt that I must have been a really bad kid to deserve how you treated me. I broke my friendship with Eve because of this. I couldn't stand to hear her father say those nice things, so I chose rather not to see her any more.'

- 'When my son first shaved, and I helped him, I wiped a drop of blood from his chin. At that moment I just realised how many times I needed your help, but you had something more important to do than to stand by me.'

The purpose of these exercises is not to tell off the person who caused the hurt. It is more important to remember the pain; to ponder why things happened as they did; to formulate our desired outcomes for the future – then, slowly, to let go of the past and even forgive. This is the ultimate goal.

2. Instead of pretending as if nothing happened, find the moral and make it part of the present

Many would like to erase the hurt and events of the past as if they had never happened, but this is not possible. This might sound strange, but I believe it is for the best. The hurts of the past not only leave a scar: they also protect and even motivate us. They are just like our wrinkles or our fingerprints. They are stories that determine who we are – they are the proof that we have lived. They are part of us; they belong to us. Have you ever wondered why at funerals a recent picture of the elderly deceased is portrayed, and not one from their youth? Exactly for the same reason: the wrinkles became who they were and were part of their life.

If we cannot wipe away the past – and neither should we try – then what should we do? It is best to find the moral of your story and build it into the present in order to make your future better. Psychotherapy has developed several methods for this, and one of the most effective is reframing. The classic story of reframing is about two friends who meet and one of them asks: 'Has your therapy worked? Do you still urinate at night?'

The other answers: 'Yes, it did work! I still urinate, but it doesn't bother me any more!'

Reframing is the act of giving a new frame of reference to a traumatic experience so that it appears in a very different light. This way, we gain a new perspective that will help us to distance ourselves from the experience and re-evaluate. This makes the 'monster' less scary so that we can handle it and set ourselves free to even discover some positive aspects of the past. I have seen a few memorable examples of reframing in therapeutic sessions.

A couple in their late thirties had sought help because of problems caused by infidelity. They told me that they had never gone through such a deep crisis before, and that they were panicking. When I asked them what kind of crises they had experienced, they started to talk about some more tragic incidents. They told of how they dealt with the loss of the wife's father, who died in a tragic car accident. They talked about how hard it had been to start all over again after a bad decision caused them to lose a fortune and bankrupted them. They also listed several smaller crises, and the common element in all of them was that they were able to overcome by helping each other. So I gave them some exciting homework. I told them that it seemed that they were experts in dealing with crises, so I asked them: 'If I were a publisher and I asked you to write a manual of how to handle a crisis, what chapters would it have? Next week I want to discuss your methods, along with the principles and techniques you suggest. Bring the outline of your manual and please write some lines explaining each chapter.' The couple did an excellent job, and our therapy was to help them to go through the steps they had outlined.

Another time, a woman in her forties sought help because her partner had left her after five years in the relationship. She had really invested a lot into those five years: her emotions, her dreams, her hopes and her money – basically everything she had. She had hoped that he would be the 'true one', but he simply walked away and swapped her for another woman. She was devastated, and when she scraped her remaining self-worth and self-respect together 'it all fitted into a small jar.' I again used reframing to assist. I told her, 'Let's imagine that your last five years were spent in a university, and you have just graduated. For a graduation, a lot of resources have to be used: time, money, hard work, emotions. . . . What if this university were a relationship university where you gained knowledge that cannot be extracted from books? What if this is you at the graduation ceremony? What would be written on your diploma?' She spent the next few weeks writing her 'diploma' and her 'credit transcripts'. She listed all the things that she had learnt about herself, about relationships and life, all the knowledge that she would take with her to enrich her life in the future. She ended up with quite a long list, and at the end she knew all her subjects by heart and started to value them as valuable lessons that she paid a lot for – lessons that would guide her in her future relationships. It was amazing to see how she grew and how much confidence she gained. At the end, she didn't remind me at all of the broken person she was when we first met.

3. Instead of minimising, forgive or ask for forgiveness

I am often surprised by how difficult people find it to ask

for forgiveness. Many believe that to ask for forgiveness is a sign of weakness and subordination, and they will do everything just to avoid it. They'd rather sever the relationship than face their partner and apologise for their sins and mistakes. The mind, however, will carry on the unfinished business, and in a new relationship the situation will be replicated in order to give the person a new opportunity for growth. I remember a couple where the man came from a previous marriage. He left behind a deeply hurt wife and a four-year-old in order to live with the new partner, who found the process absolutely normal because life was full of changes and everybody needed to adapt. Even when I asked her if she would say the same if he left her now for someone else, she answered, 'Yes, because all have the right to happiness – and if he isn't happy with me, he should find someone else to be happy with!' The man, however, found this hard to live with and protested heavily against interpreting the story this way. He repeated all the excuses to himself over and over again, yet he struggled to sleep and couldn't find peace. He became impassive and indifferent, and even his libido started to wane.

During our discussions we mapped out all the possible solutions. He couldn't return to his wife, because she had begun a new relationship and was expecting a baby. It didn't work either to minimise the problem. He was facing the consequences of leaving their daughter to grow up without the daily presence and support of her father. This seemed unfair to him, something that should not happen to any child. He had to name his feelings and thoughts. It was guilt. And guilt requires forgiveness and absolution, but how could he explain the issue to a little preschooler and ask her forgiveness? I suggested that he write a letter to his daughter as if she were in her twenties and explain to her why she had to grow up without him, and why he had decided to start a new life with a new family. He had to admit his guilt and call injustice by its name, because she didn't have a say, but would suffer the consequences. He asked for forgiveness and said he was sorry. I cannot describe how deep the emotions were that welled up while he was writing that letter, but the paper was wet with his tears. Fortunately he got to process his guilt and face his choice, and also make some decisions about how he could be more present in the life of his daughter, even if not every day. The change was profound, and the revival of his libido signalled it the most.

4. Instead of feeling indebted, let go of the unalterable and be open to a new life

As we saw in the previous story, we must face up to the past. Whatever can be set right must be, and that which cannot be changed must be relinquished. The ritual of closure can be of great help in this. For ages, rituals have been available for mankind to work through their emotions, close off a life stage and start a new one. It is not by chance that a certain script is followed at funerals, when loved ones have died. Similarly, we also follow a script during weddings to celebrate the unity of two individuals. Hurtful memories also can be released by following a 'letting go' or closing ritual. In some countries divorce ceremonies are becoming fashionable, during which the divorcing parties, in the presence of loved ones and friends, let go of each other and close off a part of their lives. Jellouschek even suggests a script that is similar to the wedding vow for this purpose: 'I accept all that you have given me. I will remember respectfully all I have received from you, and for all that I thank you. I take responsibility for my part in the breaking down of our relationship and I let you take responsibility for your part. I will respect and value you as the mother/father of our children, and I will do all in my power to co-operate with you in their care. As a spouse I let you go. Goodbye! Walk your own path, as I will also walk mine.'[5]

Other life situations might require their own rituals. One young man, burdened by his mother's suicide and the fact that he was unable to prevent it, put all the negative messages that arose out of this life event on a metal plate and then burnt it. A ritual can be used to process a miscarriage when the affected persons deal with its aftermath years or decades later. There were a couple who managed to lay down this burden by holding a symbolic funeral for the unborn baby. They wrapped several items intended for the child into a shoebox and placed it on the river Danube.

How can we know if we have put the past right?
As I mentioned, the past cannot be erased; but it can be put right and processed. This process has stages that signal where we are in the journey. By knowing these stages, we can know how far we are along the way.

Phase 1: I cannot avoid thinking of it – the events of the past paralyse me in the present
In this phase the pain is very intense, and the event feels as vivid as if it happened only yesterday. Whatever we do, read or watch on TV reminds us of the pain. In this stage we cannot concentrate and the event demands quite a large part of our emotional capacity. It is a big help if there is a friend who can stand by us and be called upon, even in the

middle of the night, if we feel we cannot make it through to daybreak. Therapy is also an option, and sometimes even medication might be warranted.

Phase 2: It hurts when it comes to my mind – I only seldom remember it, but it doesn't influence my present

This is a more advanced phase in the process, when it is not in our minds all the time. We are mostly able to concentrate on our family and our tasks; but when it does come up, it has an effect. I experienced this for a while after my grandfather died. I didn't have it in my mind all the time, but when I remembered the 'good old man' I had to step aside for a short time, and it felt good to let the loss and pain go through me. But after a few minutes I would take a deep breath and continue with my life.

Phase 3: It doesn't recall negative emotions any more – I have processed it, and built the moral into my present experience

This is a mature level that everybody should reach sooner or later. Even if we remember the event, we will not be under its influence, and will not be heartbroken. The methods and principles mentioned above will help you to get here. Let's return to the example of the death of my grandfather. I do not try to make sense of it any more – why I lost him. Instead, I'm thankful that he was with me for many years. If I pass his house, it is not the great loss that I feel, but I remember many pleasant memories from my childhood that I experienced there.

Phase 4: I'm thankful for what happened – the events of the past are part of who I am

This is a beautiful state, where all the bad that has happened receives a new meaning. At the beginning of the book I told the story of a man whose leg amputation changed the life of the family. I also mentioned the family where depression played a big role. Sometimes, even though it may sound absurd, even the worst things can turn life in a better direction, helping it to become richer and more fulfilling. It is wonderful when a sad event can be reframed in such a different way. When Viktor Frankl, the famous psychologist, was asked how he could continue to live after Auschwitz, where he lost all his family, he replied: 'I want to be worthy of the fact that I could survive.' I have to note that not all humans are capable of this, and not all life events can be reframed or redefined this way. This fourth phase should be considered as a bonus. If we have gone through the first three, we will already have done ourselves a big favour.

Summary

Everyone is burdened in some way with injuries from the past: from childhood, from previous relationships or from random, traumatic life events. These influence the present and sometimes even determine it. Whatever you have in your baggage, do something with it! No one can hide these things for a lifetime, and no one can pretend forever. The past can prevent happiness in the here and now, preventing lifelong commitment and loyalty towards a partner. It is time to face the past: to process it, to resolve it, to forgive and to be forgiven, to let go and to take responsibility!

What this all means for the three types of marriage I presented you with in the beginning of chapter 2 is summarised in the table overleaf.

The three types of marriage and dealing with the past

Superficial	Functional	Deep
The couple are not aware of how strongly their past affects their present relationship. They do not control the steering wheel; instead, the autopilot has taken over. They avoid responsibility and interpret life as fate – something that toys with them. Their motto is 'Take it or leave it!' or 'That's my luck!' They can both have many unhealed wounds.	The couple often hold the steering wheel but they are not rewriting the autopilot program. They try to work well together in the present, but feel powerless concerning their past. They believe that the past is a cross to be carried and they don't enlist the help that could improve the quality of their lives.	They have intentionally processed their past: they took responsibility for their own mistakes and let go of things that weren't their fault. They have made it to at least phase 3. Not only has the reprogramming of their own autopilot been important for them, but they also try to program the autopilot of their children as best they can.

Exercises

Answering the questions below will help you to make use of the principles presented in this chapter in your own relationship, and to practise them in everyday life. Answer these questions honestly! If you don't want your partner to see them, use a separate sheet that you can throw away if you wish to. It is important that you do not contemplate your answer for long, but that you write it down as soon as possible. The words will have a real effect only if they are pronounced or written down!

1. Map your backpack!

Unprocessed events from my childhood that have an

effect on my present life:
Unprocessed events from my previous relationships that have an effect on my present life:
Traumatic, random events that have an effect on my present life:

2. **Which events are those that most influence how you attach to your partner, how you live faithfully to him/her, and how you accept his/her closeness?**

3. **How can the following principles help you to process the events? Prepare an action plan! Be as concrete as you can!**

Instead of fleeing, face it:
Instead of denying it, make the lessons learnt part of your present operation:
Instead of belittling, ask for forgiveness or grant forgiveness:
Instead of feeling indebted, let go of the unchangeable, and be open to a new life:

[1]Henry Cloud et al, *Unlocking Your Family Patterns*. [2]Jellouschek, *Warum hast du mir das angetan?* p. 91. [3]Jellouschek, *Warum hast du mir das angetan?* p. 92. [4]Hans-Joachim Thilo, *Ehe ohne Norm?* pp. 168-173. [5]Jellouschek, *Warum hast du mir das angetan?* p. 162.

Let's make it 100%

6

I'm not happy when people take principles from business and apply them to the world of relationships without further consideration. How is this habit related to fidelity? Let me explain.

Some years ago we bought a bread machine for my mother-in-law for her birthday. The machine broke after two months; the dough blade simply stopped working. We went back to the shop with the machine and made a claim on the warranty. The shop assistant filled out the forms, and asked: 'Would you like to get your money back or would you like to get a new one?' After picking a new machine, I asked her why it was that she didn't offer to repair it. She told me that these machines were not profitable for the manufacturer to repair; it was cheaper for them simply to scrap the old machine and offer a new one. Since then I have heard the same logic applied to a broken mixer, an iron, and a sewing machine bought for my daughter for Christmas. There is no attempt to repair, only to replace. It seems this consumer attitude has become so infused into our thinking that we even tend to use it in very different areas, like marriage and family relationships. Is it broken? Simply replace! Do not bother to repair. . . .

I was watching TV ads that were being shown between the various segments of that evening's film. This time the ads promoted financial services. One wanted to convince me to buy a flat, then Christmas gifts and a car, even a graduation dinner with my children – all on my credit card. They promised to process my credit approval very quickly. I could have the credit available in under 24 hours. For this privilege I would only have to pay a 41.3% interest rate! Another advertisement declared that the same bank would be happy to receive my money and give me a full 3% interest. This made me think. When this institution wants to lend to me, they believe it is so important that they can ask for 41.3% interest. However, when I am lending them money, they offer me only 3%. Is their money better than mine?

Anyway, the point is that we seem to have learnt to expect maximum gains with minimum investment. If the bank can do this with us, why shouldn't we do this to others? If this works in the business world, why can't it work in other areas of life as well, like in relationships? It may seem unbelievable, but how many live out their relationship investing 60-70% and expecting 120-140% in return? At the end they are upset and hurt when this doesn't work. Hey, come on! Which bank will give you a £2,000 return for a £1,000 deposit? Please, if you find one, let me know!

Yet I have observed similar ideas with couples preparing to get married. They are very excited to let me know the details of the wedding: which dress they have chosen, which company is to make their wedding cake, what the bouquet is going to look like, and who is to celebrate their wedding with them. Under such circumstances I tend to say this: 'It is wonderful to see *how you are preparing for your wedding!* However, *are you putting the same energy into preparing for your marriage?*' At which point I can see in their eyes that the idea that they should get ready for the marriage puzzles them. The idea persists that it is enough to meet the true and only one, then to have a great wedding party, and all that follows will be fine. No, it will not! As Ádám Mészáros has put it in one of his presentations: 'Marriage doesn't work! It must be worked on!'

Marriage, though it has some financial functions to it, is not a financial institution; thus, many things that are standard procedures in business life will not work in an emotional covenant between a husband and a wife. For example, if I were to fund a company together with one of my friends, into which he contributes £3 million and I contribute only £1 million, he will have 75% of the investor vote and I will have 25%. The profit would also be shared in the same way, which is totally correct. This is how business works. The problem arises when someone working in the business world transfers these same principles into his marriage. Then, when a decision is to be made, he brings up how much he earns and how much he pays into the marriage, and says that because he contributes more, he should have a bigger portion of the vote. When applied, such logic can be taken to mean, for example, that the one who earns more has the right to choose the holiday destination. It might even be used to construe that they are entitled to a bonus in the form of a fling. It is very important to understand and to adopt the fact that the marriage is not a financial venture and that the spouses do not have voting rights assigned according to the financial capital they bring to the relationship. The marriage is between two equal adults, where equality is a fundamental right and is not dependent on any other factors.

Marriage gravitates towards divorce by itself

If you have ever planted beautiful flowers in a garden, or you have a well-cultivated lawn, you know that they need to be watered every day. The garden has to be designed first; then the necessary tools, seeds or seedlings need to be purchased. After the ground is prepared, the plants can be planted and cared for. And, after you have done everything well, you will have a garden in which it is a pleasure to sit and invite others to share with you. All this happens not by chance; it is the result of very intentional and hard work. If the effort is not put into the project, there is not going to be a result. Gardens do not bloom by themselves.

The marriage works like a garden. I have seen many marriages that reminded me of beautiful, tended gardens, and many more that looked like abandoned, neglected weed lots. The beautiful ones were all made that way by the intentional efforts of the couple; the weedy ones simply happened to grow like that.

It was a surprise for me that this correlation could be proved statistically. An important part of my PhD research was to measure the effectiveness of the *Connect* relationship training seminar that I had developed.[1] The participating couples filled out a questionnaire three times. I used a modified version of the Couple Checkup questionnaire that Professor David Olson had created. The first time the couples filled out the questionnaire was when they arrived at the training in order to understand the quality of their relationship. The second test was filled out right after the 15-hour training had been completed in order to see how much their relationship had developed. The third questionnaire was filled out six months after the training in order to see how much the skills and information they had learnt had become part of their relationship lifestyle. The results were summarised in a diagram where the growth of the couples' relationships becomes visible.

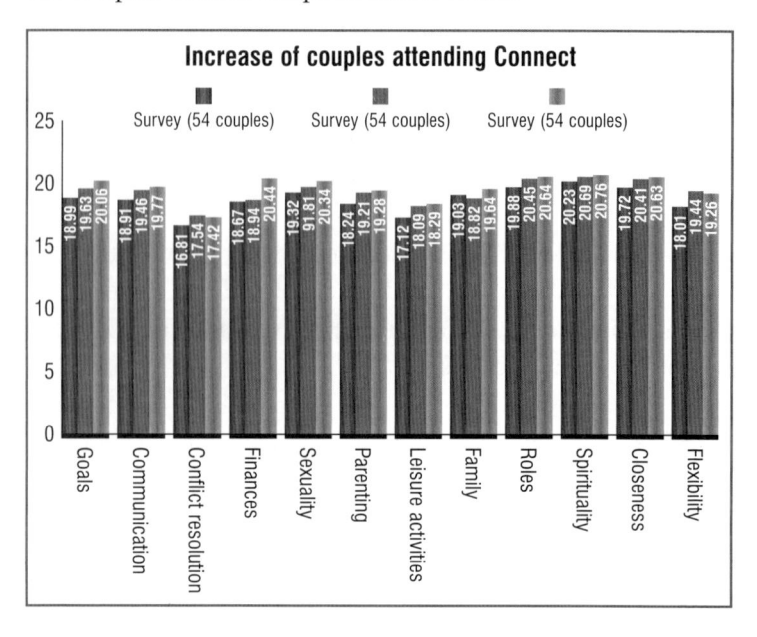

Increase of couples attending Connect

Area	Survey 1	Survey 2	Survey 3
Goals	18.99	19.63	20.06
Communication	18.91	19.46	19.77
Conflict resolution	16.81	17.54	17.42
Finances	18.67	18.94	20.44
Sexuality	19.32	91.81	20.34
Parenting	18.24	19.21	19.28
Leisure activities	17.12	18.09	18.29
Family	19.03	18.82	19.64
Roles	19.88	20.45	20.64
Spirituality	20.23	20.69	20.76
Closeness	19.72	20.41	20.63
Flexibility	18.01	19.44	19.26

The chart proves that those couples who work intentionally on their relationship during the 15-hour training, and completed the 40 couples exercises designed to strengthen their relationship, experience a gradual improvement in almost every area of their relationship. Even in areas where they didn't show improvement right after the training (conflict resolution, family and flexibility) they develop in the longer run. I'm very pleased with these results as they proved the *Connect* seminar to be the first scientifically validated relationship training in Hungary.

As with many scientific assessments, we must try to examine what would have happened with the couples if they hadn't participated in the *Connect* training. Maybe they would have achieved the same results even without the training. Maybe the values of the various relationship areas would have grown anyway simply automatically, and the results are not tied to the effort the couples put in at the training. To shed some light on this, a control group was set up, which consisted of couples who didn't participate in *Connect* or any other relationship therapy or training; they simply lived their lives. This group was made up of couples who filled out the questionnaire twice, six months apart. This way they served as a reference point concerning what happens to couples if they do not work to improve their relationship. The changes to their relationship are summed up in the following diagram.

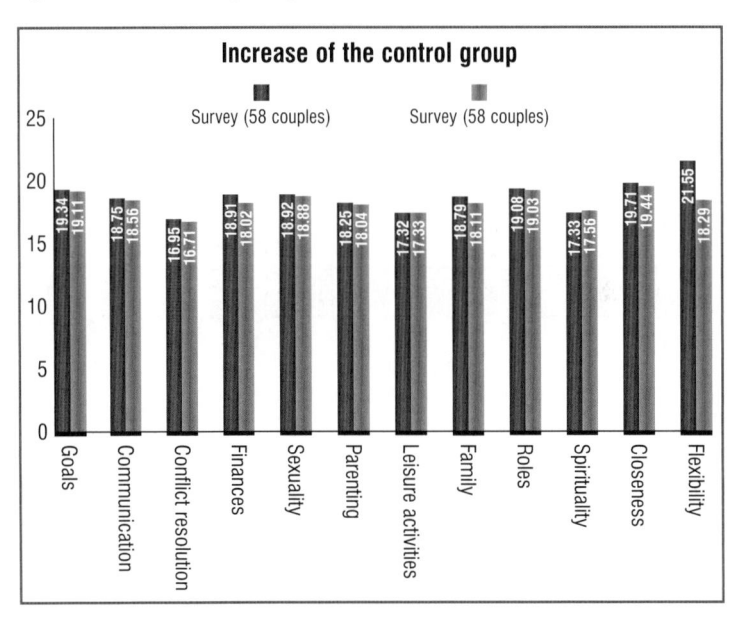

Increase of the control group

Survey (58 couples) Survey (58 couples)

Category	Survey 1	Survey 2
Goals	19.34	19.11
Communication	18.75	18.56
Conflict resolution	16.95	16.71
Finances	18.91	18.02
Sexuality	18.92	18.88
Parenting	18.25	18.04
Leisure activities	17.32	17.33
Family	18.79	18.11
Roles	19.08	19.03
Spirituality	17.33	17.56
Closeness	19.71	19.44
Flexibility	21.55	18.29

It can be observed, with two minor exceptions (spirituality and leisure activities) where you can see some positive progress, that the quality of these relationships was declining. The result corresponds to the processes in the garden, if we wait for the garden to develop by itself. As in the garden, where only the weeds will grow as the result of a natural process, so marriage will also gravitate towards divorce if nothing intentional is done to improve its quality. This can be stated as a fact based on the findings displayed in the chart.

The difference between the two groups is even more obvious if the results are displayed in the same diagram. In the diagram the achievements of the *Connect* couples – the difference between the first and the third test results – are shown in percentages. The changes in the control group are displayed in a similar manner. The difference speaks for itself:

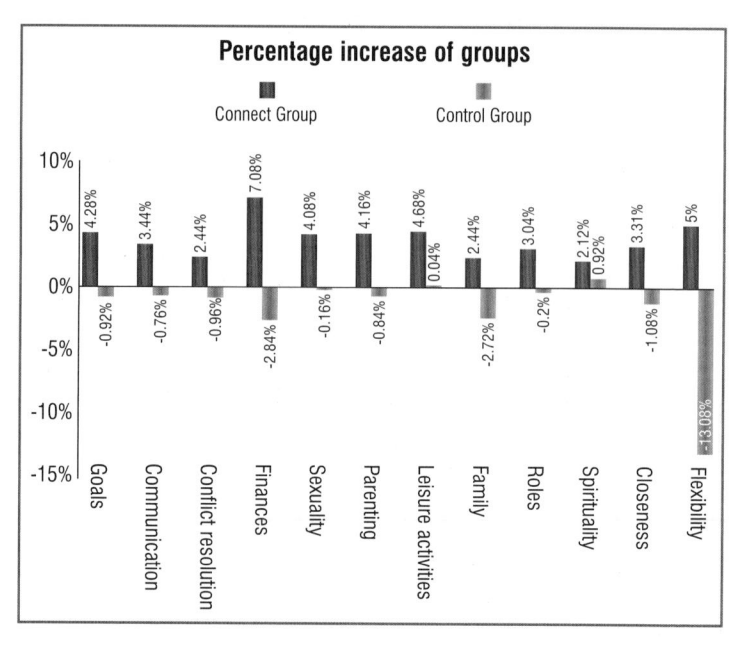

Percentage increase of groups

Connect Group — Control Group

Category	Connect Group	Control Group
Goals	4.28%	-0.92%
Communication	3.44%	-0.76%
Conflict resolution	2.44%	-0.96%
Finances	7.08%	-2.84%
Sexuality	4.08%	-0.16%
Parenting	4.16%	-0.84%
Leisure activities	4.68%	0.04%
Family	2.44%	-2.72%
Roles	3.04%	-0.2%
Spirituality	2.12%	0.92%
Closeness	3.31%	-1.08%
Flexibility	5%	-13.08%

The difference is shocking, isn't it? And it will be even more dramatic if the six months are magnified into several years or decades! There are couples who work for years on their relationship, putting 100% of their effort into it and gaining a good return. And there are other couples who for years or decades are just drifting, letting natural decline direct their relationships. Is it any wonder that one out of every two marriages ends up in divorce in most of the developed countries? The negative trajectory of a relationship points to a divorce.

Marriage enrichment as part of the family budget
Once a couple get addicted to working on their relationship, this will change their thinking and lifestyle, and will become a great inspiration to all around them. This approach will influence their decisions, plans and behaviour. One of the major changes will become obvious in the planning of the family budget.

During a premarital counselling session there is a compulsory exercise that the couple must do in order to prevent future conflicts. There is a budget planner that includes all the typical incomes and expenses that the couple must fill out. Among the expenses are three things that surprise most couples: savings, donations and marriage enrichment programmes.

To build up savings might seem self-explanatory to many; however, it is by no means the case for all couples. Statistics are really surprising. Many families do not have any savings or reserves to fall back on. Let me state, at this point, that to have savings is not dependent on the income, but on the mentality. I have met couples where both parties had high incomes, yet they had no savings. I have also met couples who lived on minimal wages, yet they amassed surprising amounts of financial reserves. There is a strict law of family finances that I also adhere to: namely, that a family need savings equivalent to 3-6 months of their regular expenses in order to maintain their living standards should they experience financial difficulty.

What about donations? Financial means are not only a privilege but also a responsibility, especially if the couple have children. If we want to raise empathetic children who have a sense of social responsibility, and who don't always want to be on the receiving end but want to contribute to society, then we need to educate them from quite an early age to be like that. There is an unbelievably popular culture of selfishness and exploitation that promotes the attitude that other human beings are only the means to an end. If we want to resist this inhuman and demeaning trend then we are obliged to involve our families in making monthly contributions to worthy causes that enhance the well-being of others.

The most exciting of these strange family budget items is, however, marriage enrichment. The money that we use for our relationship (for example, a good book on relationships, the fees for a training seminar, a candlelit supper, or a wellness weekend) may seem like luxurious expenses and a financial strain simply because there will always be other, more urgent, expenses. However, if marriage enrichment is always part of the budget, and we save intentionally every month in order to spend that money on strengthening the relationship, we will soon have a very different attitude, as this amount will generate a double profit. Firstly, we will be able to buy the book, purchase the ticket or just go somewhere without the children and not feel bad about it. Let me note here that the ideal is to have a free evening every week, a full day every month, a weekend every quarter and a week every year which is only for the couple. Secondly, this intentional ring-fencing for your relationship will also have a psychological benefit, as we are reminded every month that our relationship will not work of itself, but only if we work for it and invest in it.

The positive side effect of couples therapy

In one way a marriage therapist's work is similar to that of a gladiator. Do not worry; it doesn't involve blood! In the film *Gladiator*, Maximus, the main character, says to the others before a battle: 'Whatever comes through that door, we have more chance of survival if we work together.' This is the similarity between the jobs. A counsellor doesn't know either who will come through the door next, or how they will co-operate. Only after we start to work together will we know what pains and expectations the couple have.

Some come in as if bringing a car to the mechanic: 'There you are! This is my marriage: it broke; you are the specialist; make it work again! I'll be back when you are ready!' They are the hardest ones to work with, as they think they can be outside of the solution and step into it once all the others have done the job. Unfortunately (or thankfully), it doesn't work this way. As they are part of the problem, there cannot be a solution without them. I'm either able to convince them about that, or the process is doomed.

Another approach, which is better, but not optimal, is when the couple arrive believing that they are the ones who placed an order, and they are waiting for a solution. They are willing to work towards a solution; however, once we leave the course of action they believe is the best, and work on an area that the therapist deems important and connected to the problem, they will start resisting, and quickly let the therapist know that this wasn't part of the deal. Even if we are able to find a solution for the problem and satisfy the contract, I always have reservations after these meetings. I feel there would be more benefit to this relationship had the partners been more open. And I always have some fear concerning how long the positive effect will last in this type of marriage: whether all factors were processed, or only what the couple thought were the problems.

The most beautiful experience is, however, when during the therapy the couple not only solve their problems, but start to enjoy **their improved relationship** and discover how much power they have to further enrich it. They are the couples who will benefit more from therapy than they expected. They will become intentional in their married life and receive the tools with which to become better at managing it. These couples do not finish their work at the end of the session, but will continue to push for an even better marriage and for a happier partnership. They are the ones who will see their friends' marriages from a different perspective, and start to encourage them to work and to grow too. It is always a great joy for me when these couples come back after several years and say that they have just bought a *Connect* training voucher as a gift for their friends. I call these couples 'ambassadors of marriage enrichment'. They are the ones who know how this success tastes, and want to share the experience with others – to motivate them to grow intentionally in their marriage. The magic word is: 'intentionally'!

For a long time I was convinced that this was something obvious, something that everybody understood, but I came to realise that this is not the case. I was invited to lecture, and in the invitation letter I was asked to provide a few sentences that the organisers could use in their advertisement. In those sentences I used the word 'intentional' twice. I was very surprised, however, when the organiser sent back the text for revision, because I thought that it was well worded. The message stated that I should rewrite the advertisement and that I should avoid the word 'intentional'. Her explanation was that the word affected her very negatively in an advert about emotional relationships, as it referred strongly to the *mind* and the *will*. I had to admit that she was right to some extent. We are encouraged not to think in order to be good consumers. It sounds scary if someone encourages the opposite: for us to use logic, careful decision-making and consciousness, even in relationships. We cannot, however, get the best out of our marriage unless we are intentional.

Catch 22

It shows clearly how much danger there is in the ideology of 'let's put in 60% and expect 120% back' during therapeutic sessions that deal with infidelity. There is a phase when the cheater is torn between the spouse and the third person. This is a really hard situation for them, as they are really afraid that if they return to the spouse they will end up with the same problems they wanted to escape, and on top of that they would also lose the excitement and all the perceived potential of the developing illicit relationship. In this case they usually opt for the most secure solution: *they don't opt for anything*. They simply maintain the status quo and try to balance between the two relationships. They communicate to the spouse that they are only *observing* whether their marriage will work or not, and whether it is worth giving up the dream of the extramarital relationship for the reality of their marriage. This way they are 50% in their marriage and 50% in the new relationship, while watching to see whether the spouse will be able to deliver to their satisfaction on all of their emotional needs – 100% – or not. In this situation the cheater has divided his or her love between the spouse and the partner so that the spouse will get 50% at best. This is the extent to which the cheater is participating in the marriage, putting in 50% but expecting 100% back! This is very unfair and the attempt is doomed to fail. First of all, there is no emotional law that would allow 100% return for 50% effort. Secondly, as the attention is divided the person will not be able to take in 100% from the spouse. For that to happen, the person should exclude the extramarital partner. Let's put it this way: I'm able to take in the input of my partner as much as I'm willing to work for the relationship.

In the 1960s and 1970s the psychology experts discussed and debated neutrality a lot – the ability of the observer to stay neutral. Is it possible that someone observing a system is able to stay independent from the system itself, or will they inevitably become part of it? At first they supposed the observer to be impartial. For example, the family will continue to function in its usual way, while the therapist is able to observe them as if watching a theatre drama. This is called primary cybernetics. Later on this supposition was proved to be false. The observer (therapist) becomes a part of the system (family or relationship) to some extent as they start to interact. The observer is not just an external onlooker, but an actor influencing the story thread. For example, an audience has an effect on the actors and can motivate them to put on their best performance ever.

This is a message to all who cheat: if they believe that they can be external observers and not participants, and that they will be able to objectively decide if their marriage is able to give back 100% or not, they must let go of this idea, as they will be disappointed. Because of the cheater's half-hearted performance not even the spouse will be able to give the best performance she or he is capable of. The achievement of the 100% output is not just dependent on your partner, but is also dependent on how much you put into the relationship. And if you put 50% into your marriage, there is no way you can get much more out!

Selfishness makes anyone unfit for marriage

A Facebook message by one of my friends really hit me in the heart. The quote was this: 'Objects are to be used; humans are to be loved. The tragedy of humanity started when we started to love objects and use humans.' Whoever wrote it, it is a very true observation.

Developmental psychology divides human development into several phases, and I have found that many relationship problems stem from the fact that the person hasn't struggled through the necessary developmental crises that are characteristic for each phase. People often start relationships without ever facing the most profound questions of life: Where did I come from? Where am I heading? What is the purpose of my life? And because their self-image is ill-formed or insecure they are obsessed with themselves and don't have any free emotional or intellectual capacity to concentrate on others. For this reason they do not relate to others, but end up using them instead. After these 'others' have served their purpose such persons simply move on because the 'others' are not partners, just tools – and tools are replaceable. This is why many change their so-called partners as their interests, goals and whims mutate. All this is encouraged by the spirit of the age that sets the freedom to satisfy one's desires as the highest of all values, which then provides an ideological basis for the shedding of our personal responsibility for others.

A person who is supposed to be an adult will qualify as an adolescent if they only seek their own gain. When family and marriage are not values in their own right, but only become important to the extent that they deliver an advantage or benefit, a serious problem exists. The same is true when the person is unable to take responsibility for their problems but blames others instead. This type of person is unfit to marry. In my opinion, what makes an adult – what distinguishes an adult from a child – is that he or she is able to take responsibility and accept blame; is able to tolerate, to resist temptations, to make decisions, to persevere, to forgive and to ask for forgiveness. To sacrifice these values for fake freedom is not self-realisation but self-deception. I do not wish to give the impression that one should stick to a relationship that is damaging physically and mentally, or that anyone should settle for abuse and indignity. Not at all! A man cannot have the same approach as a husband and a father that he used to have in his teenage years. My needs are not the most important, and it's not I who need to be right all the time. Neither is personal fulfilment the most important objective in my life, nor fun more important than responsibility. A person shouldn't flee conflicts or disappointment in a marriage. A spouse shouldn't avoid challenges, but choose rather to resolve the problems, even if this is a harder road to take. It is worth it!

It may seem easier to escape a relationship, ignore your problems and blame others for the failure. But a true husband and a true wife, a real mother and a real father, know that 'ME' cannot be the most important all the time. Marriage and family are resources and values that are bigger than ME, and they are worth sacrificing and fighting for!

Summary

It is unrealistic to expect a 100% return from a relationship where we invest only 50% effort. A maximum return is realistic only if we invest 100% effort. Mature adults can be expected to make sacrifices in order to achieve something greater than themselves, and to tolerate difficult circumstances without looking solely after their own interests and enjoyment. This is also part of the investment that will bring great results. This type of behaviour will also form an inheritance that will even have a positive effect on the marital stability and happiness of the next generation.

What this all means for the three types of marriages I presented to you at the beginning of chapter 2 is summarised in the following table.

The three types of marriage and the 100% investment

Superficial	Functional	Deep
The couple are not conscious of what is happening in their relationship. They expect it to improve by itself. If this doesn't happen, they conclude that it is the result of picking the wrong person as a partner, and will try to change the partner in order to fix the problem.	The partners make sacrifices, and because of their family patterns or their religious values they stick to each other even if their relationship is full of challenges. However, they lack the skills and tools to improve the relationship. They rarely ask for help, and, as long as they can, they will try to resolve the problems themselves.	The partners learn to invest in their relationship as a result of premarital counselling or a successfully managed crisis. They both participate as mature adults in maintaining their relationship. They value their family more than their personal desires, and they are happy to make sacrifices for it. The priority of their relationship can be seen in their timetable and budget.

Exercises

Answering the questions below will help you to make use of the principles presented in this chapter in your own relationship, and to practise them in everyday life. Answer these questions honestly! If you don't want your partner to see them, use a separate sheet that you can throw away later. It is important that you do not contemplate your answers for too long, but that you write them down as soon as possible. The words will have a real effect only if they are pronounced or written down!

1. What is your understanding of the functioning of a relationship? Where are your convictions coming from? The following questions will help you to draw your own relationship map:
   - My parents made their marriage work by: _____
   - What I want to preserve from their praxis: _____
   - What I do not want to preserve from their praxis: _____

2. The following questions will help you discover resources that enable you to put 100% into your relationship:
   - Next month we will dedicate this amount to use to enrich our relationship: _____
   - Our relationship is important and we want to dedicate time to spend together, just the two of us. We do not want to use this time to resolve differences, but to strengthen our relationship. Taking our family responsibilities into account we will dedicate the following time for each other:
     - Weekly: _____
     - Monthly: _____
     - Quarterly: _____
     - Yearly: _____

We are going to use the budgeted money for the following activities: _____

[1] Gábor Mihalec, *The Border Areas of Christian Counselling and Psychotherapy in Marriage Counselling*, PhD dissertation, pp. 308-353.

How to build an atmosphere of trust and intimacy in your marriage

7

There is a biblical story that makes my heart beat faster every time I read it. At the dawn of human history, right after the story of creation, we are introduced to the first human couple living in a harmonious relationship: 'Then the LORD God made a woman from the rib he had taken out of the man, and he brought her to the man. The man said, "This is now bone of my bones and flesh of my flesh; she shall be called 'woman,' for she was taken out of man." That is why a man leaves his father and mother and is united to his wife, and they become one flesh. Adam and his wife were both naked, and they felt no shame.' (Genesis 2:22-25, NIV.)

They were naked and felt no shame. They had nothing to hide, in both a literal and a figurative sense. They lived together with the greatest openness and trust that people can ever experience. This idyll now seems far away and unreachable, even if everybody desires to experience the same state of soul and body. Yet we are afraid to drop our defences and look into the eyes of our partners, and to open up to each other and make ourselves transparent and vulnerable.

When two people bind their lives together they also place

themselves in each other's hands. A process of growth should take place as the partners trust each other more and more, with fewer and fewer reservations, accepting each other's decisions and values and judgement. In this process, the feeling of love helps a lot, because it is easier to trust a person who is emotionally close to us and makes us feel comfortable and important.

Once, while I was visiting a Croatian national park, we had to leave our car in the car park and take a bus ride to a waterfall some kilometres away. The trip was certainly an experience to remember, and a good exercise in trust. The driver who took us to the waterfall was a kind, happy man who greeted the passengers one by one, whistled songs while driving, and waved happily to the passing drivers. Despite riding on a difficult road full of dangerous curves and deep ravines, I felt safe. However, coming back we had a driver who was obviously in a bad mood and didn't seem to care about the safety of his passengers. He was on his mobile phone the whole time, and gave the impression he had gotten out of bed on the wrong foot. Even though we were on the same road coming back, being driven in a similar bus, I feared for my life.

What do we need in order to learn to trust someone? According to trust experts, there are several factors that build up trust: competence (an experiential conviction that the person knows what they are doing and is able to get things done); consistency (the person has repeatedly, and over a long period, proved their trustworthiness and predictability); care (the person has empathy and acts in the interest of others, and we can rest assured that they are on our side); honesty (being sincere and open, the person is able to discuss both negative and positive issues without being unkind, and is able to consider the pros and cons of a suggestion, not only the ones he likes); authenticity (the person will say and do whatever they really think and feel).

During dating the couple get to know each other in several life situations, and these experiences foster the feeling that they can depend on each other. This feeling will influence the decision as to whether we will want to live with the other person for the rest of our lives. We observe how inventive and adaptable the person is in difficult situations, like on a trip in a foreign country. We also experience how the person relates to his or her loved ones: for instance, with parents and grandparents and siblings during a family celebration. We get to see how the person deals with a host of everyday situations.

Slowly the decision will be made to marry, and the couple start to plan their future together. Our expectations come from the experiences of dating, and sometimes our trust falters. This can happen on several levels. On the level of competence, we may realise that the partner is not as competent as they seemed to be. There are decisions where they either freeze or make hasty, faulty decisions. Maybe the person is very strong when it comes to theory, and is respected at work, but is not very good in practical things. As a result of this, then, the daily running of the relationship will weigh more heavily on one party and the power sharing will be unbalanced. In a situation like this, a wife once told me: 'I have been carrying this man on my back. I want him to walk on his own feet now.'

Distrust can also arise in the area of consistency, especially if a 'yes' is not really a 'yes', and 'no' is not always 'no'. Where promises are not kept, the loss of confidence can be very damaging because it will cause a constant sense of doubt in the partner's mind. 'Will he come and pick me up as he promised?' 'Can I really trust her and count on her in this situation?' The one who leaves the other in the lurch might not even realise how negatively this can be perceived. They may be convinced that they can be trusted: after all, it was only twice that they failed to keep a promise. The partner, however, may feel differently, and based on those two incidents will feel let down and very unsure of any further promises.

Care is a very important part of every relationship, as it makes the partner feel special to the other person. 'I'm important to him; he even does this for me!' If this feeling is lost, the relationship loses the component that makes it unique when compared to other relationships. Infidelity is especially hurtful in the area of care, as it is a betrayal of the uniqueness of the relationship. I have heard many times from the betrayed spouse: 'I have taken care of him; I cooked his favourite dishes. How was he able to leave with that . . . ?' 'I was looking after her tiniest wishes; I worked myself to death to provide a good life for her – and she got into a relationship with her boss.'

To lose trust because of a lack of honesty has an even greater negative impact. To lose faith due to a lack of consistency – either because of forgetfulness or the conspiracy of unfortunate circumstances – is one thing. However, to be disillusioned over a partner's honesty suggests that they have done something premeditated. The person knew what the right choice was, but chose to act differently. After this type of disappointment, doubt will linger for a long time: 'Was he really there where he said he would be? Is he going to meet the person that he said he would meet?' If one partner loses authenticity, the other one will feel that this partner is a different person to what he or she shows on the outside, and in many cases the partner will be rejected.

Trust and infidelity are so closely connected that we cannot say where one ends and the other starts. John Gottman's research has produced tangible results in this area: 'The disloyalty is not always expressed through a sexual affair. It more often takes a form that couples do not recognise as infidelity. In my lab, partners will insist that despite their troubles they have been faithful to each other. But they are wrong. Betrayal is the secret that lies at the heart of every failing relationship – it is there even if the couple are unaware of it. If a husband always puts his career ahead of his relationship, that is betrayal. When a wife keeps breaking her promise to start a family, that is also betrayal. Pervasive coldness, selfishness, unfairness, and other destructive behaviours are also evidence of disloyalty and can lead to consequences equally [as] devastating as adultery.'[1] After researching infidelity for a long time, Gottman is very direct in his opinion: 'By analysing the anatomy of this poison, I have figured out how to defeat it. I now know that there is a fundamental principle for making relationships work that serves as an antidote to unfaithfulness. That principle is trust.'[2]

The more enduring trust is in a relationship, the more willing the partners are to take care of each other, and the more they are willing to do for each other. The couples who have a high level of trust will be excited and happy about the same things. If one of them has success, the other will be happy as well. If one of them is hurt, the other one will be sad. With couples where trust is reduced, the parties are often happy for things that hurt the partner.

Gottman developed a test that makes it possible to measure trust between the partners. The test can be found in his book, *What Makes Love Last?* on pages 16-21. It will help you obtain an objective picture of your relationship's trust level. It is best if you both fill out the test and compare your results.

Trust is not a constant entity within us that either exists or doesn't exist. It is dynamic and will change constantly in the relationship. Therefore, we have to work intentionally to develop it, and it is possible to make it grow.

1. Cultivate a culture of respect and admiration

The more positive things we say about our partner; the more intentionally we search for things we can be proud of in them; the more lovely characteristics we find – the more we will be drawn to them. This will also make us more attentive, and we will see things that are important for our spouse. I'm always surprised by those who give very personal presents to their partners. Such acts are a statement that they know the other partner intimately and that they are in tune with them. A man once told me this after a crisis that reduced his trust: 'For fifteen years I was able to buy her very personal presents. This Christmas, however, no matter how hard I tried, I couldn't come up with anything. At last I simply went into a shop and bought something because this is customary.' How well do you know your partner? Can you list his or her favourite films, books, music? Do you know which concerts your partner would like to go to, or who her or his favourite relative is? Do you remember the names of any of her or his childhood pets?

2. Don't live together with 'scrappy' things

It is hard to trust someone in a relationship which harbours unresolved issues. These are the issues that create that feeling of 'OK! OK! But . . . there's another side to that!' If we have caused any grievances in the past then we should deal with them. Let go of the past; forgive, and ask for forgiveness.

3. Resolve the conflicts that can be resolved!
This is very similar to the previous point. The difference is that these are not only shadows from the past that influence our relationship, but conflicts that feed on the present situation. Conflicts cannot be avoided, but they must be resolved with the prospect of coming closer in the relationship.

4. Have glass pockets and glass hearts
If we trust someone we have nothing to hide. Hiding finances is not an option. Lies cannot be part of the relationship, even if they are 'only' withholding information. They will undermine trust, and how can we trust someone in whom we are unwilling to confide the truth? Would it be a surprise if I were to receive the same treatment from my spouse? There is no place in a marriage for misinformation. Just as politicians are expected to have glass pockets, married couples are expected to have glass hearts!

5. Exercise positive fidelity!
Howard Clinebell distinguishes between positive and negative faithfulness.[3] The negative faithfulness is motivated by outside factors, and it is based on fear of consequences. The positive faithfulness is motivated by internal factors, and is based on mutual love and respect. The person doesn't cheat on the partner because they love them, and the relationship is of much greater value than a few hours of fleeting excitement. Professor Emőke Bagdy found that we project negative or positive

faithfulness on our partners. For example, if a wife constantly hears from her husband that one day she will fall in love with someone else, and that she will not be able to remain faithful if infidelity presents itself, she will likely reason this way: 'You see, it happened: just as you kept telling me. This was expected, so why wouldn't I have grabbed the opportunity?' And she will be more inclined to commit infidelity. However, if she is receiving messages from her husband like: 'I trust you! I believe you have a strong character. You would never give up on our marriage just for the sake of a fling,' she will feel secure. In this situation she would tell herself: 'Pull yourself together, and get out of here! You are trusted and you cannot violate that trust! How would you face your husband? How would you look in the mirror? You cannot ruin, with one bad decision, all that you have built up!'

6. Do things together just for the sake of being together

If I think about the persons in my life whom I can really trust (thank God, there are a few like this) then I see one thing they all have in common. I have spent a lot of time with them in one or another phase of my life, and our friendship and trust is the natural byproduct of this time spent together. This is true of marriage as well. If we spend a lot of time together then we get to know the person and we get to trust them. Marriage is in need of leisure time spent together – time when we are not together to do something, but only to be together with our friend.

An effective medicine against a headache

I cannot count how many couples I have met for whom sex has become a bogeyman, something threatening. So much hurt and bitterness have become attached to sex that even just hearing the word will start a stress reaction in their bodies. Sexuality is a defining part of true intimacy. For me the book of Michele Weiner Davis was a revelation.[4] She states this about the role of sexuality: 'Sex is an extremely important part of marriage. When it's good, it offers couples opportunities to give and receive physical pleasure, to connect emotionally and spiritually. It builds closeness, intimacy, and a sense of partnership. It defines their relationship as different from all others. Sex is a powerful tie that binds.'[5]

Yes, this would be ideal, but . . .

A young, well-educated, well-off couple are sitting in front of me with pain written over their faces. The wife has called me to book the appointment, but when I ask why are they here she points at the husband, signalling that it is his turn to speak. Anyway, she cannot speak, as her tears have stifled her voice. The husband tells me that this relationship is their first and only one, and that it was love at first sight and that they still love each other ('at least my wife is really clinging on to me'), but sex doesn't work for them. During the first one and a half years everything was fine, but then the wife had a gynaecological problem and received hormonal treatment. As a result she put on 15 kilos and since then she won't appear naked in front of him, and refuses all his initiatives towards intimacy. It doesn't matter what he tells her: how sexy and desirable he still finds her, and that he loves her as she is. The woman simply cannot let go of the idea that she cannot be loved, and the husband cannot seem to change this conviction. A year has passed since they last had sex. In order to preserve his self-esteem, the husband distanced himself further and further from her so as not to get hurt too deeply, as he felt that his wife didn't love him any more and that he was not desirable enough. He also distanced himself emotionally.

The wife realised the danger in the situation when her husband first pronounced: 'I do not want to hug you; it doesn't feel right.' She understood immediately how profound the effect was that the situation was having on her husband. She had thought that her withdrawal would not affect their relationship, because the husband always initiated sex once she let him come closer ('because men are like this'), which made her feel secure in rejecting his advances. She felt that there was nothing to lose, as her husband was always on 'standby'. But, at that moment, she knew that this wasn't the case any more. Their relationship was now in so much danger that they might not be able to get out of the ditch they were in. As a result of that realisation, she started to initiate sex, but now it was his turn to refuse: he had lost his interest in her.

This story is typical in many ways. We know from statistical research that 20% of couples are having sex less than ten times a year. Also, low sexual appetite is one of the leading causes for people to seek sexual therapy. Naturally, what is little and what is a lot is very subjective. The therapists agree that the normal range is between once a day and once a month. This is quite a broad range. For example, if the wife wanted to have sex once a week, but the husband once a month, then the wife's sexual appetite would be four times larger than her husband's. But there are couples where the man would like to have sex every other day and the wife twice a month. The research of one of my university classmates showed that satisfied couples had sex two to three times a week. This might provide a reference point, but statistics are sometimes useful and sometimes not. 'Most couples with a desire gap have disagreements on how much sex is enough. The person with less desire thinks that his or her spouse is oversexed. The person with more desire thinks just the reverse. Perhaps you've tried to settle matters, as couples in my practice have, by enquiring about the average number of times per week or month married people of various ages make love. Although these data exist, they're useless, because what one person or couple finds satisfying is grounds for concern or divorce in another person or couple. Statistics don't tell you anything about you or your marriage.'[6]

Sexual appetite is not a pre-programmed drive that was finalised at our conception, but it changes from time to time. The couple in question didn't have any problems at the beginning of their relationship: they were in tune with each other. Then something happened that changed it, first in one of them and then in the other. However, if sexuality can change for the worse, then it can also change for the better.

Most people are convinced that 'headaches' only haunt women. In the film *What women want*, the boss of a PR company, played by Mel Gibson, wants to build a full advertising strategy based on this stereotype. This motivates him to write the following line for a painkiller marketing campaign: 'So mild and gentle that you can take it even when you're faking a headache.' Yes, women are thought to have headaches, but it is hard to imagine men having them, as they seem to have three things on their minds: sex, sex and sex. Against this cultural background, if the man happens to have problems with his sexual drive, he will hide it at all costs. Weiner Davis states that the man with a headache is one of the most closely protected secrets of our age.

Women, as we saw in our story, often suppose that men want to have sex just to satisfy their own desires and lusts. It doesn't matter with whom: they just want enough, and then they are content. They suppose that the state of mind and the feelings are not important to men, only the sexual gratification. To suppose this is a colossal mistake! It is true that men experience sexuality differently to women, but they have much deeper motivations than instant pleasure. For men, sex is an important communicational channel through which they receive the message: 'Someone wants me; someone wants me just as I am; I'm valuable to someone.' I'm always shocked when, in a conversation, I ask men who are sex-dependent what they are chasing, what they really want from sex. The consistent answer I receive is this: they want to feel longed for and accepted (or, rather, included) just as they are. This means that the man who is rejected by his wife is going to be deprived not simply of sexual satisfaction, as sex is not simply a sexual act, as many degrade it to. 'Sexual intercourse is the ultimate symbol of intimate human relationships. The act of intercourse can allow us to experience in the most intense way possible our deepest biological, emotional, and spiritual strivings, and at the same time allow us to share these feelings with another person. . . . Sex can be an act, but it can also be a highly meaningful metaphor.'[7]

The partner with the smaller sexual appetite rules the couple's sexual life. It might seem that this person is always on the defensive and in a difficult position, as she or he has to resist the siege. To the contrary, however, this is the person in charge, controlling how often they make love. This might make the other partner feel vulnerable, and sends them this message: 'Sex is not that important for me; I do not want it. I know that you want it, because you are like this, but I'm comfortable without it. This is the situation: you have to accept it, and I also expect you to be faithful and not to pursue intimate relationships with others.' This sounds unfair. Naturally, I do not condone the idea that this situation is a permit to commit infidelity. But I do understand that many situations like this get to the point where the other partner will seek intimacy with others. I have heard this many times from both men and women: 'I'm serious about marriage. Faithfulness is a core value for me. I reserve intimacy for my partner. But what do I do if my partner doesn't want it? Am I to reserve my intimacy in the long run for someone who doesn't want it?'

This is not fair! While the partner with the smaller appetite can reasonably expect self-restraint from the other one, and that this tension is to be resolved within the framework of their marriage, the partner with the bigger sexual appetite can also reasonably expect the other one to be more accommodating of his or her needs. Is this an intentional area as well?

Desire starts with a decision. It is ultimately your choice if you want to have an exciting, vibrant, physically and emotionally fulfilling sexual life with your spouse, and to achieve that you must be willing to act. Take responsibility and be the initiator.

The course of sexual togetherness is displayed in the so-called arousal curve. If you have read my book, *I Do*, you might remember the graphic as well. This curve is separated into different phases. In the desire phase the thoughts are increasingly occupied with the idea of 'things that might happen between us'. In this phase a pleasant meal, candles, music, an intimate chat or a bath can do wonders. . . . This phase is followed by the excitement phase. At this point physiological reactions showing excitement will kick in. The reactions function as a green light: they indicate that the partners are open to continue. The foreplay is a vital part of this phase, which helps the partners to get synchronised and prepare for the next phase, and that includes the intercourse. The next phase is called the plateau, where the level of excitement is high. The name stems from the emotionally and sensually elevated state of the partners and its constant and continued high level of sexual arousal. The plateau phase ends in two shorter but equally significant sub-phases where signals of the inevitable orgasm appear. This leads the couple into the orgasmic phase, the most famous of them all. This is the ultimate pleasure and joy for both sexes, with visible and audible signs. After the orgasm comes the most neglected phase, the resolution, which should be treated otherwise than it is, because it is very important.

And now to our major point! According to Weiner Davis, in the cases of persons with a low sexual drive, the first two phases are either in the wrong order or they have simply disappeared – the desire and the excitement phases might be missing. If this is the situation then men and women shouldn't be worried: they work totally normally; only they do not start the process easily. The problem is not with their sexuality, but only that they have difficulties in getting into the mood. Once they start on the road, they will be able to experience the plateau, the orgasm and the resolution – but only if they start slowly. Davis suggests that they follow the Nike principle. Why is it called Nike? Actually I had a long dispute with my son about which is the better sports brand: Nike or Adidas. Even if I'm all for the brand with the three stripes, I have to admit that Nike is the best in one thing. The company started the most successful advertisement campaign of all times in 1988. You know their slogan as well: 'Just do it!' In ten years this slogan helped them to push their global market share from 18% to 43%. The slogan is still around on stickers, T-shirts and sports bags. How does this apply to human sexual life? Masters and Johnson already advised in the '80s: you do not need to burn from desire to consent to sex. In other words: just do it! Maybe desire will not come spontaneously. Maybe your day was stressful and it is more in your thoughts than is sex. However, if you want to choose to support your marriage, be part of the game. Maybe this doesn't sound as spontaneous and romantic as you might expect, but hey, if it works, just plan sex ahead and go along with your spouse. Start with the second phase! Once the stimuli are in place the rest of the process will be enjoyable, normal and healthy. Many times the most intimate and enjoyable and memorable sex acts start like this. Weiner Davis states that he has saved several marriages with this method, and I can second him on this statement. Many couples have given feedback that endorses it as useful advice. The interesting observation they make is that once they had a regular sexual life, they even started to have the desire prior to the stimulus. It is certainly worth a try!

Eliminate the barriers
Joyful sexuality doesn't grow by itself. This is only a myth that we have believed because the porn culture made us believe in it. It looks so easy: two persons look at each other, they feel an irresistible desire, they move closer, they go for a kiss, they rip off their clothes and have the wildest, most exciting, and most satisfying sex, obviously reaching orgasm at exactly the same moment. After the sex act they introduce themselves so as not to feel like strangers any more, and both go on their separate ways. In real life, there are a myriad of internal and external factors that are able to negatively influence our sexuality. It is worth paying attention to these factors as you try to eliminate the barriers

to good sex. Bryan Craig names these possible causes in a concise list.[8]

Physical: fatigue, pain (headache, backache, arthritis, painful intercourse), feeling unwell (nausea), poor health, chronic illness, some medications, hormonal changes, breastfeeding, menopause.

Psychological: lack of emotional well-being (stress, guilt, anger, worry, resentment, sadness, frustration, depression, shame), poor self-esteem, feelings of sexual inadequacy, poor sex education, negative sexual attitudes, poor body image, lack of pleasurable sexual thoughts and fantasies.

Relationship: lack of loving attraction, sexual difficulties, limited sensuality, lack of affection, companionship, fun and romance, lack of trust, unresolved jealousy, insecurity (lack of commitment), poor communication, lack of intimacy, lack of respect, boundary intrusions (e.g.: work demands, in-laws, children, social activities, hobbies).

Situational: lack of privacy, poor atmosphere in lovemaking (e.g.: lack of time, distractions from kids, TV, phone).

As you can see from this list, sexual togetherness needs preparation. The couple need to synchronise this, and it sometimes needs to be planned, just as during dating the dates had to be planned and agreed upon. In those days, it didn't happen that the man went to a park because he felt like that and suddenly his girlfriend just mysteriously appeared there. That sounds like a fairy tale. In reality, the man had to invite the lady and agree on a suitable time for both. It gave the woman time to prepare, to get ready, to think about the evening, and to feel good even before the date. It isn't spontaneous. Yet it works just like that. Why shouldn't the married couple fix dates for their intimate hours as well?

Ádám Mészáros, a mediator, has worded a very interesting idea that still escapes the notice of many: 'Let's cultivate a clear conscience towards our partner!' Let's imagine a beautiful clean room. Now, imagine you made a mess in it: the walls, the carpet, the furniture, the pictures – all ruined. Would you still enjoy being in that room the same way as before, or would you avoid it? Most people would avoid it, even if the room is not to be blamed: it didn't do anything wrong. We avoid it because we did something to mess it up. Relationships work the same way. Unless we have a clear conscience towards our partner, we will try to avoid her or him. It will be our own conscience that will try to put distance between us, as when in his or her presence we start to remember what we did. This is one reason why I do not believe that infidelity can be maintained in secret without damaging the relationship. It is also one reason why the cheater finds it so hard to find their way back to their spouse, even though the person who was cheated on actually has more reasons to keep their distance. Maybe the infidelity will be kept in the dark, but our conscience will still be in the partner's presence and a distance will build up between us. Let us be protective and keep a clear conscience towards our spouse.

Craig also lists some influencing factors that will help you to experience joyful sexuality.[9]

1. **A clear focus.** Sexual experience is not about performance, but it is about personal satisfaction in an intimate closeness. The two shouldn't be confused. Our world is all about performance and achievement, and this

spirit scrolls into the bedroom and leads to stress, anxiety and failure. The couple need to refocus on their personal experience.

2. **A positive attitude.** The negativity is fed by multiple sources. It can come from one's prudish upbringing, or a religious conviction that condemns sexuality, or previous bad experiences, or simple misinformation. Wherever it is coming from, it will take away the joy from the wonderful gift of sexuality.

3. **Adequate knowledge.** The sexually satisfied couples know how sex works and are aware of the arousal curve of the human sexual response. They also know each other's bodies very well; know what excites their partner; and what the partner's likes and dislikes are. They are able to discuss their desires and fantasies, emotional needs and even fears. It is amazing how misinformed couples can be, not even aware of such basic information about their partners. I will always remember how one lady told me that they did not discuss sexuality as her husband had bestial leanings and kept asking her to do things that would damage her self-esteem, which she was simply not willing to do. Because she brought up this issue several times, I was forced to ask the husband what it was exactly that he was trying to make her do. But he was so ashamed that it was obvious he was not going to tell me. She did it anyway: 'I'll say it! It is not I who should be ashamed of myself! He wants me to be on the top!' Yes, you read it correctly – and I had the same look on my face as you probably have on yours. The moral: collect knowledge, talk about sex, watch some videos, or at least read the *Song of Songs* from the Bible. And please, do not read or watch porn, as it is not sex, but a cheap parody that is not suitable to inform you about real human sexuality.

4. Accept responsibility. A man once told me in tears that his girlfriend had left him, and that he now needed to collect the strength even to walk. I asked him what he would need in order to get better, and he answered that he needed a new girlfriend, as it is that which makes him function because he needs to feel loved. He said he couldn't live alone. He was very surprised when I told him that as long as he thought like this he shouldn't get involved, as it would be unfair towards the lady. Everyone is responsible for their own happiness and emotional well-being. This responsibility cannot be transferred to anyone else. Every time he put this responsibility on another person, it wasn't because he loved her, but because he was using her. It might have sounded harsh, but this man had to be confronted with the fact that he first needed to take care of himself. Our happiness is closely related to our willingness to accept responsibility for ourselves and our behaviour.

5. Communicate desire. Good communication is key to a good sexual life. Do you talk about your desires? About your sexual fantasies? Are you free to tell your partner what you would like to have happen during sex? These are so vital that I have dedicated a separate chapter to this topic.

6. Enjoy mutuality. Sex is not a one-way street. It is not just about what my partner can give me, but also about what I can give to him or her. If this attitude becomes routine then it will increase our sexual pleasure. Sex cannot become a commercial activity where one provides the service and the other consumes it. Mutuality is necessary for intimacy, and good sex is based on mutual affection, respect, passion and care.

Summary

Based on the research of Gottman, we can state that the more trust there is, the more protected the relationship is from infidelity. But trust is not a closed mechanism: it can grow stronger or weaker. If this is true, why not make it stronger?

We have also examined the factors influencing sexual life and found an effective medication: 'Just do it!'

What this all means for the three types of marriages that I presented to you at the beginning of chapter 2 is summarised in the following table.

The three types of marriage in relation to trust and intimacy

Superficial	Functional	Deep
The trust level of the spouses is changing rapidly: thus, their intimacy is showing extremes as well. They have sex, but do not make love. If they have sexual problems, they do not know what to do. Extramarital affairs can happen frequently, but, even if they are loyal to each other, they would more likely experience it as a negative loyalty than as a positive experience.	They trust each other and are committed, but they are not really happy. Sexuality is surrounded by deep scars and pain, and they do not want to talk about it. Their sexual life is monotone and routine, and they find it difficult to spice up their relationship. They blackmail or manipulate each other with sex. They are more likely to have a negative loyalty than a positive one.	The relationship of the partners is based on mutual love, respect and a deep friendship. They understand that for a good sexual life they need to invest time, honesty and a little creativity, so they are patient and do not capitulate because of little problems. They are open to change and are happy to serve each other. They practise positive loyalty and project it on each other.

Exercises

Answering the questions below will help you to make use of the principles presented in this chapter in your own relationship, and to practise them in your everyday life. Answer these questions honestly! If you would rather your partner didn't see them, use a separate sheet that you can throw away later. It is important that you do not contemplate your answer for too long, but that you write it down as soon as possible. The words will have a real effect only if they are pronounced or written down!

1. I highly recommend that you use a short test about your sexuality in Dr David Olson's book. It will give an overview of your sexuality and tell you where your strengths are and what areas should be developed. David H. Olson and Amy K. Olson, *Empowering Couples: Building on Your Strengths* (Minneapolis: Life Innovations, 2000), pp. 132-133.

2. In the area of trust, the test of Dr John Gottman can be a great tool to understand yourself and your partner. John Ma Gottman and Nan Silver, *What Makes Love Last?* pp. 16-21.

3. Analyse the script of your sexual life!

The following questions will help you to reflect on your very own arousal curve. Write down the usual experience, then what you like in it and also what you would like to change.

Desire phase:
- How does this usually happen? _____
- What do you like in it? _____

- What would you like to do differently? _____

Arousal (foreplay) phase:
- How does this usually happen? _____
- What do you like in it? _____
- What would you like to do differently? _____

Plateau phase:
- How does this usually happen? _____
- What do you like in it? _____
- What would you like to do differently? _____

Orgasmic phase:
- How does this usually happen? _____
- What do you like in it? _____
- What would you like to do differently? _____

Resolution phase:
- How does this usually happen? _____
- What do you like in it? _____
- What would you like to do differently? _____

[1]Gottman & Silver, *What Makes Love Last?* p. XVII. [2]Gottman & Silver, *What Makes Love Last?* pp. XVII-XVIII. [3]Howard J. Clinebell, *Growth Counseling for Marriage Enrichment*, p. 23. [4]Michele Weiner Davis, *The Sex-Starved Marriage. Boosting Your Marriage Libido: A Couple's Guide* (New York: Simon & Schuster, 2003). [5]Michele Weiner Davis, *The Sex-Starved Marriage*, p. 8. [6]Michele Weiner Davis, *The Sex-Starved Marriage*, p. 25. [7]Peter Rutter, *Sex in the Forbidden Zone*, pp. 62-63. [8]Bryan Craige, *Searching for Intimacy in Marriage*, p. 115. [9]Bryan Craige, *Searching for Intimacy in Marriage*, pp. 119-121.

Kill the parasites 8

In the influential film *Fireproof* (2008) there is a part about the parasites: 'Watch out for the parasites. A parasite is anything that latches onto you or your partner and sucks the life out of your marriage. They manifest usually in the form of addictions like gambling, drugs or pornography. They promise pleasure, but they grow like a disease and consume more and more of your thoughts, time and money. They steal away your loyalty and heart from those you love. Marriages rarely survive if the parasites are present. If you love your spouse you must destroy any addiction that has your heart. If you don't, it will destroy you.'[1]

A prosperous and attractive couple who have children are sitting across the desk from me. The man is the owner of a successful car showroom. The wife has a shop with two employees that is prospering despite strong competition. For both of them this is their second marriage; they love each other and are committed to the relationship, but have come close to ending it. Judging from the outside they have every reason to be happy. Looking from the inside of their relationship they are desperate. When I ask them why they have come to see me, they tell a patchwork tale of issues such as trouble with the in-laws, time management problems and failed conflict resolution. I have a sneaky feeling, however, that these are not the real causes, and that we need to dig deeper. Five minutes before our session is due to end, the wife makes a comment: 'Oh, one more thing! I do not know if this is relevant, but my husband is a porn addict.' The husband nods, confirming the information, but from his face I can see that he feels deep shame and hurt. During the next session we discuss the details of his addiction and how it has affected their relationship. I learn that during his first marriage he struggled with another addiction, to alcohol, but that after a successful detoxification programme he never drank again. I also get to know that his present addiction is a ritualistic process that follows a recurring script with detailed actions. When he switches on the computer, as soon as he hears the cooling fan, an automated thought process kicks in, and it ends in compulsive masturbation supported by porn sites. After that he feels guilt and shame; then comes the lie about urgent work he has to do at 11 o'clock at night, and the very embarrassing explanation as to why he doesn't want to have sex. . . . Despite all the negative backlash this brings, his lust and excitement are so strong that they overwrite all logical arguments and the situation repeats itself night after night.

After discussing the factors playing a role in his addiction, we collect strategies to prevent similar situations and to break the compulsive cycle that repeatedly sucks him in. At the next meeting he happily tells us that he hasn't watched porn since our last meeting. He is very excited, and tells me about all the rules he has set up and how he managed to get over his porn addiction when he was most severely tempted. Then he notes: 'I have started to smoke again, but that is something different: I can control it!'

This story illustrates something that is generally

characteristic of addictions: secrecy. Porn and its companion, masturbation, cause the person to feel ashamed, and they try to hide it. The person knows that he or she has just taken sexuality out of the marriage context and started to live in a parallel universe. This world needs to be locked away from everybody, because if he is caught he will lose face and reputation, his relationships will suffer, and he might even lose his job and livelihood. However, the keeping of that secret also comes at a very high price. It is not just about the time and energy wasted on the acts instead of being used for work or for the benefit of the relationship, but also the energy used for the frequent lies and dubious explanations that are needed to conceal the deeds. As most of the lies are told to the spouse, the guilt and the shame will be even bigger, and they will soon be accompanied by fear. This fear will force the person to withdraw a bigger part of him/herself from the relationship and become less transparent and knowable. With this behaviour the person will deprive the marriage of the exact benefits that motivate its existence: self-surrender and self-disclosure. The secret life continues to demand a bigger and bigger portion of his or her life, and takes over priority from real life. In an extreme situation the addict might end up committing suicide. Actually, 17% of porn addicts attempt suicide and 72% contemplate it.[2] Just for reference: Dr Jekyll has to kill Mr Hyde in order to preserve his identity.

Ritualistic nature. The power of rituals can be seen by observing parents and children when it is bedtime. Those children who repeat the same routine every evening experience these acts as a chain of events that prepare them to fall asleep: supper, shower, pyjamas, tooth-brushing, bedtime story, prayer, goodnight kiss, falling asleep. The whole chain of events is already activated by taking the first step without even thinking. At supper the child is not sleepy at all, but at tooth-brushing he yawns frequently, and by the time of the goodnight kiss the child is usually fast asleep. Rituals are supposed to achieve exactly this automatism. A ritual is a predictably recurring series of acts that is burnt into the mind as automatic behaviour that triggers a desired physiological and psychological response. There aren't supposed to be any links between brushing one's teeth and getting sleepy, but the ritual links them together. As the body learns that tooth-brushing is only three steps away from falling asleep, tooth-brushing starts to produce sleepiness. The ritual is a great tool in the hand of the parents in order to encourage the children to form healthy habits. However, the same mechanism can easily work against us to ingrain unhealthy and destructive habits. The sexual addictions have a well-defined pattern or script. The voyeur, the person who finds sexual gratification in watching others, will always follow the same route, at the same time, in the hope that he can see someone naked through the window without being seen. A person suffering with a compulsive masturbation problem will always visit the same web pages in the same order, just as he follows the same moves to see if he has closed the door, or not. . . . This helps us understand why the simple sound of a computer fan can cause erection.

Symptom migration and stacking. The sexual addiction rarely exists alone. Many who are affected will have some other addictions as well, either at the same time, or in turns. As we saw in the story, the man previously had an alcohol addiction, and after giving up porn he started to smoke. The research clearly shows that the sexual addiction is rarely the only addiction the person will have. Thirty-eight percent of sex addicts will struggle with eating disorders like binge eating. Research also indicates that a common secondary addiction is that of drugs and/or alcohol: 42% are drug addicts. Fifty to seventy percent of cocaine addicts are also sex addicts. Some research on a thousand-strong sample group showed that only 13% of sex addicts admitted to having only that one addiction.[3] The major questions then are: What motivates these addictions? What do the addictions replace? Why does the person have to drink, smoke or masturbate?

Alienation from the partner. Sexual addiction alienates the spouse in every case. It may not seem likely at the beginning, and the addict will find plenty of seemingly logical and believable reasons to justify his conduct. 'I'm not hurting anyone. I'm not even cheating on my wife with another woman.' 'This is only cybersex, only electrons; it is made up only of 0 and 1 digits; this has no effect on reality.' 'I'm working so much and I couldn't relax in any other way. Everybody has the right to release their tensions. This is my way. I need it in order to function better in my work and family life.' 'Our marriage doesn't work, and I do not get what I need for my sexual life. I'm doing this to protect my marriage. It is far better than going to a prostitute or having an affair.' As you can see, at this level the self-justifying reasoning tries to make out that the partner is benefiting from the addiction. To think this way promotes a dangerous lie that will build a wall between the spouses, even if the dependant uses this as a mantra and eventually comes to believe it.

When sexual addictions are examined, we are touching on an area inside infidelity that holds even more secrets than its already secretive parent category. Even the experts are locked in a debate as to what we can know with certainty from this area. There are experts who deny that it is even a sexual addiction; others describe it as a symptom; and some give it a diagnosis and write thick books about its successful treatment. I have many references to the pioneering work of

Patrick Carnes. Carnes is not only one of the first authors to write on the subject, but he also provides useful therapeutic suggestions that are authentic. He became famous by successfully treating public figures, and every major book on the subject quotes his original work and research.

What counts as an addiction?
This is the first question we need to answer. What should we have in mind when we talk about addiction? Which behaviours can be called healthy, and which are the ones that are not normal any more, and can be called pathological? As mentioned already, there are experts who do not accept the existence of sexual addiction, so most health insurers also refuse claims to treat patients with this addiction. However, there are many couples who suffer because of the effect of sexual addiction and it can be argued that it does play a role in divorces.

Carnes defines addiction: 'While our society is shifting to a more open attitude towards sexual expression, we still view the amount and kind of activity as a matter of personal choice. For the addict, however, there is no choice. No choice. The addiction is in charge. That addicts have no control over their sexual behaviour is a very hard concept to accept when the addicts' trails have left broken marriages and parentless children or, worse, victims of sexual crimes. Therefore, there are no neutral responses to sexual compulsivity.[4]

To compare sexual addiction to drug addiction is justified, especially if drugs are not limited to chemicals infused into the body from outside, but inner biochemical materials are also included. As we have defined earlier, the brain produces significant chemicals that will serve as a reward, and they also strengthen attachment to the person or item that helped to achieve orgasm. For the same reason some experts suggest that we should use the expressions 'exogenic' (infused from the outside) and 'endogenic' (produced in the body) drugs.[5] The suggestion is based on the fact that it doesn't matter if a drug is administered from the outside or produced internally, if the effects and the result are the same.

The sexual addiction can be viewed as an abuse of sexuality, similar to drug or alcohol abuse. This means that instead of using sexuality as it is intended – namely, to build trust and attachment between the spouses; to strengthen self-esteem so that the person is able to accept responsibility for his or her actions and emotions; to share grief and joy; and to develop fellowship – the addict uses sexuality in a way that results in the very opposite. The addiction creates mistrust, lower self-esteem, blaming, isolation, the shifting of responsibility to the partner, and broken fellowship.

What are the levels of sexual addiction?
Sexual addiction can be arranged into three levels that share common characteristics but also have their differences. However, these subgroups are not persistent in the structure, but will change as they gain more influence over the life of the addict. It is a similar process to the one we observe in alcohol addiction: the intake increases constantly to achieve the same effect. Sexual addiction can, therefore, be grouped as follows.

Level one
This level includes behaviours that are socially widespread and accepted, sometimes even protected by law, and no one would think of calling them addiction. However, just because these acts are legal doesn't mean they are either beneficial or ethical. There are many legally accepted acts that are downright harmful to us, but because of short-term

enjoyment and a financial benefit society accepts them. For example, everyone can read on cigarette boxes that 'Smoking kills!' yet tobacco is readily accessible. Persons on the first level are rarely satisfied with one particular act, and usually combine the behaviours listed below. Because an addiction comes in phases – for example, one week of an intensive and active phase, then a lull of three weeks – the person believes that he or she has things under control. Also, as these behavioural patterns are widespread and exercised by many others, the addicts convince themselves that there is nothing wrong with their behaviour. However, the level of isolation and hurt is growing and it starts to signal that not everything is OK. The behavioural forms of stage 1 are usually the following.

Masturbation. Masturbation is a part of normal human sexual development. We discover it as we learn about the sexual functions of our body, and begin to understand our masculinity and femininity. There are many views on masturbation and they vary between two extremes. One extreme is the view promoted by the sexual revolution and in sex therapy, that without masturbation the person gives up on self-discovery and personal development, and that there is no danger or negative effect associated with masturbation. The other extreme usually comes from a religious perspective and is based on moral reasoning. It states that our inability to avoid or renounce masturbation entirely is a feature of our sinful nature, and an indication that we are unable to rule over lust. Sometimes physiological explanations form part of the reasoning, like the dropping zinc levels which cause memory problems and are supposed to be connected to frequent sexual activity. There also are views that limit sexuality to procreation.[6] I believe the truth is somewhere between these extremes – neither on the side of excessive practice, nor on that of a guilt- and repression-inducing, moralising approach. For the addict, the masturbation is compulsive. The person is driven to masturbate up to several times a day, making it the centre of his life. Even the smallest frustration might start the urge, and the addict must then look for a safe place to soothe himself or herself. At the same time the addict will drift further away from their partner, as the act will strengthen the notion: 'I do not need you; I can give myself all that is important. I can even give sexual pleasure to myself.' As a result, the person will give up on cuddling and other displays of emotion, thereby reducing their sexual life to intercourse.

Compulsive sex. Another distinctive behaviour is where sex plays a disproportionately large role in the marriage. In this way an important part of the relationship will be subjected to the sexual needs of the addicted partner, and the quality of the relationship will be measured by the frequency and performance of sexual acts. However, in relationships where performance is overemphasised, the sense of joy, freedom and playfulness will diminish. At the point where the partner cannot perform any longer or simply refuses to do so, the addict will turn on the computer and get online. The lost excitement is supplemented in chat rooms, in secret emails, and in other ways; all of which means that the time spent online to get to know others is time taken away from the spouse, as well as being a source of growing humiliation.

Staring, pornography and topless bars. While many men may turn their heads to look briefly at a passing woman, the addict continues to stare, sometimes causing him/her or others to suffer accidents. Teenage boys are often caught paging through magazines full of naked women, but if an adult man takes one off the shelf at a petrol station it becomes suspicious. All three phenomena can be traced back to a single common cause: the desire to experience excitement with someone who hasn't consented or doesn't even know about it, without having to invest the usual effort. The addict watching pornography gains pleasure by watching another person or a group of persons. Those frequenting topless bars are willing to leave anonymity behind. They avoid affairs and the act of cheating, but try to gain enjoyment out of gazing at naked women.

Prostitution. At this point the addict steps out of the virtual world and realises his fantasies with another human being. Prostitution being a paid service excuses the client from having to invest emotionally in the 'relationship', which would otherwise be expected in healthy sexual relationships: the client doesn't need to accept the partner or meet the partner's needs. However, prostitution is very costly. It is not only that the danger of contracting a sexually transmitted disease could cost a lot, but also that the possibility of getting caught increases. The financial burden to meet the ever-growing demands of the addiction is also going to heavily impact the family budget. The lies will of necessity also multiply as the addict struggles to conceal his activities.

Anonymous sex. This is in essence the same as prostitution, except that it is not a paid service. Two persons agree to mutually benefit sexually without accepting responsibility for each other, or getting involved in any other way.

Level two
At the second level there are some socially unacceptable behaviours that are generally prohibited by law. There is also another thread that connects them all: someone is forced into a humiliated and exploited position, but, because no physical attack is involved, most of society doesn't care. Victims are

blamed and belittled and the addict is considered a harmless fool instead of a dangerous patient. These acts may be considered infantile and comical rather than harmful in some jurisdictions, but not everywhere. The behaviours listed below belong to this level.

Exhibitionism. According to its diagnostic definition: 'A recurrent or persistent tendency to expose the genitalia to strangers (usually of the opposite sex) or to people in public places, without inviting or intending closer contact. There is usually, but not invariably, sexual excitement at the time of the exposure and the act is commonly followed by masturbation.'[7] I was taught in my childhood that I should be wary of the unshaven old man in the long coat who would sneak around, ready to 'flash' in an unexpected moment. This was the usual description of an exhibitionist, but things have since changed. An exhibitionist can be of any age, with very different clothing and of either gender. An exhibitionist may go to public spaces – for example, into shopping centres – with his fly left open, or wearing jeans with strategically cut holes. It is also becoming a phenomenon that exhibitionists leave the curtains open while changing or taking a shower. Carnes mentions a special type connected to driving. Some exhibitionists now drive with their pants down, and just getting into a car can trigger the ritual, just as the porn addiction is activated by the sound of the computer's operating system or fan. Several addicts have reported that this addiction has caused traffic collisions. An exhibitionist can spend up to six hours a day on these activities. They may create alternative identities in the fear that someone may recognise them and expose their identity at their workplace or in their neighbourhood.

Voyeurism. Its diagnostic description is: 'A disorder characterised by recurrent sexual urges, fantasies, or behaviours involving observing an unsuspecting person who is naked, disrobing, or engaging in sexual activity. A paraphilia characterised by repetitive looking at unsuspecting people, usually strangers, who are either naked, in the act of disrobing, or engaging in sexual activity, as the method for achieving sexual excitement.'[8] A voyeur is a person who is looking for situations where he or she can stare at naked body parts. Other behaviours are often part of the symptoms, like the use of pornography and the frequenting of topless bars where the addict can enjoy their obsession without being considered a voyeur or having to make personal contact.

Exhibitionism and voyeurism are often combined in the same person, and the connecting link is the masturbation. The addict tries to get close to a person – for example, to hide at the person's window – and have an arousal and ejaculation without the observed person realising what is going on outside.

At the second level several other things could be listed, like phoning strangers and using obscenities or sexually provocative language and behaviour in real life, or inappropriate touching.

Level three

The acts included in the third level of sexual addiction are condemned by society and prosecuted under the nation's laws. The sentences are harsh and will usually include prison terms. Such acts may even be condemned in prison by their fellow inmates. These acts violate the law and other persons in the most reprehensible manner and are committed against the most vulnerable people. They are gross violations, and the following list includes the most common behaviours that belong to this third level of sexual addiction.

Child molestation and incest. Child abuse is a subject

that is frequently discussed in books and should be discussed even more.[9] This abuse has many forms, and sexual abuse is one of them. A child learns how to relate to others through its parents. If the parent sexually exploits the child, it plants the idea in the mind of the child that sexuality is part of every relationship, and this will encourage the child to eroticise its own behaviour. Sexuality will thus become a part of relationships where it doesn't belong. The sexual addictions and compulsions will be inherited from generation to generation, and none of them has such a damaging effect as does child sexual abuse. Incest means that the sexual exploitation happens between persons who are related. It is thus surrounded by the deepest feelings of shame and guilt, and will poison the victim's life from within. The exact numbers are not known, but the estimates are already bad enough. This type of behaviour can often be traced back at least four generations once investigated. The pioneering research of Dr Vincent Felitti is especially significant in this area. It shows that childhood sexual abuse will result in self-destructive behaviours, which lead in turn to a shortening of life expectancy by an average of 20 years. The results of this research were labelled as one of the biggest medical discoveries of the early 2000s.

A similar effect to that of incest and child abuse can occur when a professional person in a position of trust (medical doctor, psychologist or priest) exploits a client whom he or she should have healed and protected. As someone working in a helping profession, I'm deeply troubled by this and will dedicate a full chapter to the topic at the end of this book.

Sexual violence. It is the most tragic expression of loss of control when someone takes advantage of his or her physical power and forces another person to have intercourse. Many times over, these victims may be forced to suffer similar trauma to what those abused in their childhood have experienced. The perpetrator will also change and might end up as a serial abuser after having tasted power. I hope that none of the readers of this book have had to experience such a terrible ordeal.

Important conclusions concerning the phases of addiction

After introducing the three levels of sexual addiction I would like to sum up this chapter with some important observations.[10]

The sexual addiction at each level is painful and has to be taken seriously. Society might differentiate between certain acts and tolerate some more than others, but addiction is a loss of control and it is destructive and painful in every case.

Deviant behaviour doesn't necessarily indicate the presence of an addiction. Deviant behaviour can occur without an addiction. The common element of all deviant behaviour is the risk element: there is a wish to violate the rules and the norms of society without being caught, so as to escape the punishment.

All three levels of addiction can be found among people with different personalities, among men and women from all ethnic backgrounds and socio-economic strata. For this reason the addict cannot be profiled as a certain type. Interestingly, female perpetrators are judged more leniently than male perpetrators, even if they cause deeper feelings of shame to their victims.

The addicts move between the different levels of addiction. A person on the first level will eventually move on to the second level, where he or she will choose between the acts of levels 1 and 2 based on availability and the risk factor.

The actions of sex addicts are connected to the effects

of their other addictions. As we have seen before, sexual addiction is rarely a solo addiction and is usually accompanied by other addictions.

The different levels of addiction are summed up by Carnes in Figure 1.[11]

Levels of addiction		
Level of Addiction	**Behaviour**	**Cultural Standards**
Level One	Masturbation, compulsive relationship, pornography, prostitution, and anonymous sex	Depending on behaviour, activities are seen as acceptable or tolerable. Some specific behaviours such as prostitution and homosexuality are sources of controversy.
Level Two	Exhibitionism, voyeurism, indecent phone calls, and indecent liberties	None of these behaviours are acceptable.
Level Three	Child molestation, incest and rape	Each behaviour represents a profound violation of cultural boundaries.

The path to healing

The sexual addictions are easier to prevent than to heal, as are other addictions. However, it is already a bit late to discuss prevention in many of these cases. At this moment, therapy is the necessary option. Healing from sexual addiction is not only a difficult process for the addict but also challenging for

Figure 1.

Legal Consequences/Risks	Victim	Public Opinion of Addiction
Sanctions against those behaviours, when illegal, are ineffectively and randomly enforced. Low prioritisation by enforcement officials generates minimal risk for addict.	These behaviours are perceived as victimless crimes. However, victimisation and exploitation are often components of them.	Public attitudes are characterised by ambivalence or dislike. For some behaviours such as prostitution there is a competing anti-hero image of glamorous decadence.
Behaviours are regarded as nuisance offences. Risk is involved since offenders, when observed, may be actively prosecuted.	There is always a victim.	The addict is perceived as pathetic and sick but harmless. Often these behaviours are the objects of jokes that dismiss the pain of the addict.
Extreme legal consequences create high-risk situations for the addict.	There is always a victim.	The public become outraged. Perpetrators are seen by many as subhuman and beyond help.

the therapist. It is recommended only to those professionals who have researched the topic and gained field experience with an experienced sexual therapist, and who have solid values. The therapy will pursue several avenues.

What kind of unprocessed traumas might have remained from the past? There are often unprocessed struggles with sexuality from teenage years that the addict might not remember any more. I have encountered several cases where the person only got to know as an adult that their father molested her or him at kindergarten age. Because this experience was very painful the addict's memory repressed it, while the family treated it as a taboo and never spoke about it. The person may have been conscious for decades that something was wrong with her: that she had urges she couldn't control or that her relationships kept failing.

What are the false beliefs behind the addiction? Cognitive psychotherapy is partly based on the concept that our life is not primarily determined by what happened, but by what we think about what has happened to us. For this reason a significant part of the therapy is spent on uncovering the false and damaging thought patterns of the addict, and swapping them for thoughts that can help them to achieve healthy living free of self-destruction. Carnes has observed that the faulty core beliefs of sexual addicts can be grouped around four major topics:[12] '(1) I am basically a bad, unworthy person. (2) No one would love me as I am. (3) My needs are never going to be met if I have to depend upon others. (4) Sex is my most important need (addicts), or sex is the most important sign of love (co-addict).' Successful therapy will overwrite these faulty beliefs and replace them with the following positive messages: '(1) I am a worthwhile person deserving of pride. (2) I am loved and accepted by people who know me as I am. (3) My needs can be met by others if I let them know what I need. (4) Sex is but one expression of my need and care for others.'

How does the person seeking help think about himself? This topic is closely related to the previous one, but it has a different emphasis. It focuses on what addicts think about themselves and their actions. Is the addict able to understand their personhood and their deeds? If these two are seen as one and the same by the addict, then it will sound in the mind as if 'I am the problem' – however, if they are seen as distinct entities then it will sound as if 'I have a problem.' The addiction is easier to grasp if we place it outside of the person. Besides, it is easier for the addict to recognise their own virtues as well, because the person should have other positive values beside his or her addiction. These values are something to be proud of, but the addiction is covering them up. If only they were visible to them, they could use the virtues as resources to fight against the addiction.

How does a person control unwanted behaviour? What can be done with the urges, and what types of security protocols can be put in place to guard against these acts? This is a plan made in co-operation with the therapist that has to be accepted by the addict. It includes, for example, a trusted individual from his family or friendship circle with whom the addict can share his or her struggles and whom the person can phone when the urges seem overwhelming. There are also computer programs that filter content or send notifications to the trusted friend if pornographic content is opened. The friend can help the addict to be accountable. To list the specific steps is also a requirement for controlling the addictive behaviour. For example: 'I will go to bed every night together with my wife/husband and will not use the computer alone.' Or, 'I will not drive home on the road where prostitutes hang out.'

How to handle the shame and the guilt of the past? The events of the past cannot be brought to closure and the future cannot be looked upon with hope if someone feels that they have a debt because of past wrongdoing. This sense of debt will resurface again and again in the guise of guilt and shame. The shame stems from the fear of what close relatives and friends will say if they get to know about these deeds. The guilt comes from the realisation that they have exploited others and caused them hurt and humiliation. These feelings have to be dealt with. Many report feelings of relief once they have admitted their acts and do not have to be afraid of being exposed any more. Others tell of how good it felt to at last have their affairs in order again. They talk about how good it felt to at last look their partners in the face without fear, and how good it is for their self-respect that they now receive love despite people knowing about their bad deeds. Naturally, the partner's co-operation is necessary in order for this to happen, and the return to this peaceful state isn't always a smooth ride. Unfortunately, in reality (in vivo) this cannot be achieved in all cases. For example, a voyeur will not knock on every door to say sorry wherever he was looking through the window in the middle of the night. It would only cause feelings of insecurity in his victims, and make them fearful of staying home alone. In these situations another way (in sensu) must be found by the creative therapist. Whichever way, it must be dealt with, because a professional cannot belittle the importance of shame and guilt, for that would hinder the addict's growth into a mature person.

What kind of future does the person imagine for himself? In my opinion, this is something very important, because the addiction takes control to such an extent that the addict is unable to imagine his or her own life without it. The therapist should help the addict to find and imagine an alternative future where there is no place for the addiction. This is a much higher goal than just to make it through thirty days without slipping back into the addiction. If the person makes thirty days without addiction, what then? Most will relapse. However, if the person has a picture of the future in front of him and knows what he wants to achieve in five years' time, where he wants to be and with whom he wants to be, then whenever there is a danger of relapse the addict will find something to fight for. He will ask the question: 'Is it worth sacrificing my future for half an hour of excitement that this addiction can give me?'

Among the therapeutic models there is one that most professionals would recommend as one of the most effective steps to get rid of addiction. This method is based on the group sessions of Alcoholics Anonymous, and it is modified to suit the needs of self-help groups run for sex addicts. The common group experience will be more empowering to those who have to fight the same monster.

The twelve steps are the following:[13]
1. We admitted we were powerless over addictive sexual behaviour – that our lives had become unmanageable.
2. We came to believe that a Power greater than ourselves could restore us to sanity.
3. We made a decision to turn our will and our lives over to the care of God as we each understood Him to be.
4. We made a searching and fearless moral inventory of ourselves.
5. We admitted to God, to ourselves, and to another human being the exact nature of our wrongs.
6. We were entirely ready to have God remove all these defects of character from us.
7. We humbly asked God to remove our shortcomings.

8. We made a list of all the persons we had harmed and became willing to make amends to them all.
9. We made direct amends to such people wherever possible, except when to do so would injure them or others.
10. We continued to take a personal inventory, and when we were wrong we promptly admitted it.
11. We sought, through prayer and meditation, to improve our conscious contact with God as we understood Him, praying only for a knowledge of God's will for us and the power to carry that out.
12. Having had a spiritual awakening as the result of these steps, we tried to carry this message to other sex addicts and to practise these principles in our lives.

Let us address the religious element of the twelve-step programme for a moment. Although the twelve-step programme emphasises the importance of the presence of God, it doesn't limit the concept of God to that of one denomination. This is what the expression 'as we understood God' refers to. It isn't the goal of this programme to turn non-believers into believers, but rather to help the addict to exchange their personal beliefs that were built around the addiction for healthier and more positive ones. What does this personal belief of the addict mean? There are many similarities between religion and addiction, which Freud pointed out in a rather negative way. Both emphasise the dependence of a person on a stronger power (religion points to God; addiction, to a drug, experience or act); both have recurring ritualistic acts (in religion the worship, the prayer, the Bible reading; in addiction the different acts described in the three levels of addiction); and there is a compulsion to repeat the act (in religion the person doesn't want to lose closeness to God; in addiction the person doesn't want to experience loneliness, anxiety, insanity, etc.). Besides the similarities there are huge differences, as big as between theology and geology, or heaven and earth.

The addiction makes one sick, while balanced religion makes one healthier and more relaxed (this is the part Freud missed completely). This is why the programme aims to cure addictions by changing personal beliefs. The addict will first discover and expose their secretive, enslaving addiction, and then they will adopt a personal religion that will give them strength and a sense of dignity that will improve their experience of life. Later, the relationship with God will serve as a model of how to build up a relationship with, and how to trust, other people. This helps to break the power of the secretive world over the real world, and the person will gain a pride that will make it possible for them to build a new identity.

Recovered alcoholics say that they are still alcoholics, only they do not drink any more. These twelve points likewise suggest that recovery from the sex addiction will be a lifelong process that will include challenges and constant battles; but also solidarity with fellow addicts and a commitment to having a deeper understanding of sex addiction, as if they have found a new goal and mission in fighting against addictions. I would like to believe that the recovered addict doesn't have to remind himself of where he came from and what needs to be avoided. It was good for them to leave the painful past behind and live a relaxed new life without having to be afraid of relapse.

How is sex without addictions and destructive abuses and tendencies? The acronym of sex addicts' self-help groups, SAFE, gives a great summary: not Secret, not Abusive, no bad Feelings afterwards, not Empty of relationships. In other words, a healthy sexual life will be intimate but not secretive; it will display deep attachment as part of a personal relationship; and it will be free of the abuse and power struggles manifested in subordination and coercion. It will also be free of feelings of shame and guilt, and it will not take from the relationship, but enrich it; will not empty it, but fill it.[14]

What is wrong with porn?

It happened when I was about 14 years old. I was travelling with a classmate to a neighbouring town to take my highway code exam when we had a daring idea while passing a newspaper stand. At home I would never have dared to buy a sex magazine, simply because the newspaper guy knew my mother and I was afraid he would report me: but here nobody knew who we were, so the risk was around zero. We pooled our money and started to walk towards the news stand, while quarrelling along the way about who should ask for the magazine, and in the end my friend won. The lady at the counter surprisingly sold us the magazine without any question or comment. We sat down in the park, and started to page through the magazine with big eyes and great expectations. When the time came for us to take the exam we were faced with our next dilemma: what to do with the magazine? We had no bag, and our pockets weren't big enough to hide it from the examiner, so we came up with the solution of hiding it under a bush and then returning after the exam to collect it. We even agreed on one of us keeping it for a week before the other one could have it. We went off to take the exam and, surprisingly, both of us failed. I do not know if it means anything, but this was the only test I have ever failed during my entire life. Never once during primary school, high school, university, my PhD course or on any other occasion have I ever had to repeat an exam. But I failed that time! And, if that weren't enough, when we returned to the bush, the magazine was missing: someone had taken it. Actually, it was taken by a drunk guy in his fifties who was sitting on a bench nearby, enjoying our magazine! We never dared to reclaim it. . . .

Since then almost 30 years have passed. However, I can still vividly remember the front page of that magazine, several pictures, and even some titles. I experienced the same thing from which I would like to protect fourteen-year-old schoolchildren during sexual education classes. Pornographic content is like internet spyware: it uses the memory of our computer to serve others. They get our data, our user habits and our interests, maybe even our bank data – our passwords and credit card numbers. And at the end these programs congest our computers so much that we cannot use them as intended any more. The system becomes so slow that we will even struggle to type a simple text document, and eventually it will crash. The frustration will be so high that we will have to take the whole useless thing to a computer shop to be cleaned and reinstalled.

Pornography has a similar effect on our minds. The pornographic images will burn into our memories and overload some areas. At first the affected person doesn't even notice this extra load, but as time passes it becomes more burdensome. The system starts to slow and the person is less and less able to perform basic chores; it starts to malfunction and they might experience a meltdown. And all this for someone else to make a profit! The similarities are obvious, but there is also a huge difference between our mind and a computer. A computer disk can be erased and the system reinstalled, but our mind cannot be erased and reinstalled. Whatever we install, it will stay there.

By the way, what do we talk about when we discuss pornography? Pornography is an ancient Greek expression that consists of two words: porno (from *porneia*: adulterer, prostitute) and graphia (*graphé*: to note, to portray, to document) = documented prostitution.

Pornography makes so much profit that it is hard to ignore. It is present everywhere, and can be accessed from anywhere. According to conservative estimates the porn industry generates 100 billion USD income a year, and many blame the industry for a 32 billion USD sex-slave trade that victimises mostly children and women. Three thousand and seventy-five dollars are spent on pornography in every second just in the United States alone. Forty million people are regular porn consumers in the US; 70% of 18-24-year-old men and 66% of 20-40-year-old men regularly visit pornographic sites on the net. One in every six women says that she has a problem with porn addiction and the largest amount of internet traffic on porn sites is generated between 9am and 5pm – normal working hours! Fifty-six percent of divorces now list a 'compulsive interest in porn' among the reasons for ending the relationship. People become porn consumers at the average age of 12, and nine out of ten children (between 8 and 16) have already seen porn on the net.[15]

The challenges of porn can be summarised in the following four points.

It destroys. Pornography makes its consumer an addict, estranges the person from their real-life partner and fills the mind with content that distracts them from the realities of everyday life. Pornography deprives children of their childhood and its innocence by exposing them to verbal and visual effects that they cannot digest with their limited mental and emotional resources.

It degrades. Porn takes away women's dignity and degrades them into objects that are at the disposal of men to use as sexual tools. A research group compared 304 scenes from the fifty most popular sex videos and found 3,375 verbal or physical instances of aggression. Seventy percent of the aggression was committed by men and 94% of the violence was targeted at women. This means that during each sex scene men hit and verbally assaulted women 7.68 times on average.[16]

It devalues. Victor Cline, a clinical psychologist working at a clinic that specialises in helping porn addicts, says: 'The first change that happened was an addiction effect. The porn consumers got hooked. Once involved in pornographic materials, they kept coming back for more and still more.... The second phase was an escalation effect. With the passage of time, the addicted person required rougher, more explicit, more deviant and "kinky" kinds of sexual material to get their "highs" and "sexual turn-ons". It was reminiscent of individuals afflicted with drug addictions.... *The third phase was desensitisation. Material ... which was originally perceived as shocking, taboo-breaking, illegal, repulsive, or immoral, in time came to be seen as acceptable and commonplace.* ... The fourth phase was an increasing tendency to act out sexually the behaviours viewed in the pornography, including ... frequenting massage parlours.'[17] It is interesting to note that there are researchers who have concluded that those who watch porn regularly will feel less compassion towards victims of violent crimes, especially victims of sexual abuse.

It exploits. The porn industry is not at all about appreciation of sensuality and free sexuality, as it is often advertised, but about profit. For bigger profits the industry is willing to callously exploit its workers. For those working in the porn industry the average life expectancy is as low as 36.2

years because of sexually transmitted diseases and suicide. Chlamydia and gonorrhoea infection are ten times higher among them than in the average population, and drug addiction is also significantly higher among porn workers.[18]

To sum up the problems of porn, we can say that it is not only a problem because it perverts, but because it will also make one insensitive. It doesn't liberate sensuality, but cripples the emotions instead. It doesn't make one behave like an adult, but is more likely to cause regression and emotional deformity. Instead of widening a person's horizons, it will cause moral and emotional blindness. Instead of freedom it will enforce bondage.

Dr John Gottman noted that there is little chance to develop sexual addiction if the couple watch the porn together in order to turn on their sexuality.[19] However, we still have to decide whether, once we know the tragic statistics cited above, we can in clear conscience support the porn industry by using its products.

Summary

The parasites are addictions that absorb our attention and time. Their presence slowly makes the addict turn their back on loved ones: on spouse and children. In this chapter we have dealt especially with a special type of parasite called sexual addiction. We have come to understand its levels of involvement and the way to begin healing from it. I hope that the information presented here will never be needed in your life. However, if you have a friend, who has a friend. . . .

What this all means for the three types of marriage I presented you with at the beginning of chapter 2 is summarised in the following table.

The three types of marriage and the parasites

Superficial	Functional	Deep
The couple follow the social trends and don't question their effects on their relationship. Whatever is legal is acceptable. They have several forms of sexual addiction, such as porn or prostitution. (There is often a background problem of childhood sexual abuse.)	The couple mostly follow conservative customs and values. Even if there are some parasites present in the relationship, they hide them from each other. They struggle with shame and guilt.	The couple consciously invest in their relationship, so parasites rarely appear. If they appear, they can be openly discussed between each other, and they can count on each other to fight addiction.

Exercises

Let's talk about parasites.

'Watch out for the parasites. A parasite is anything that latches onto you or your partner and sucks the life out of your marriage. They usually take the form of addictive gambling, drugs or pornography. They promise pleasure, but they grow like a disease and consume more and more of your thoughts, time and money. They steal away your loyalty and devotion from those you love. Marriages rarely survive if parasites are present. If you love your spouse you must destroy any addiction that has your heart. If you don't, it will destroy you.' Alex Kendrick, *Fireproof* (film), 2008.

1. Have you got things/hobbies/persons in your life on which you spend more time/money/passion than on your partner/spouse/children? If so, what are they?
2. Is there a history of addictions in your family of origin? If so, what was their effect on your family?

3. Do you know any success stories in which your forebears were able to defeat an addiction? If so, how do these stories affect you?
4. If a day of your life were recorded on video and your kids/partner were to see it, what parts you would you be proud of and what parts would you be ashamed of? What would you change so as to take all shameful things out of your day?
5. If you found a magic wand, and you could change one event in your life, what would it be, and why?
6. If you were stuck in a lift with a sexual therapist who dealt with addictions, and you could ask the person anything, and you had time for the conversation, what would you ask?
7. If you were to catch your child watching porn on the net, what would you say? What are the values you would uplift, what arguments would you list, and what steps would you take in the future?
8. Examine your sexual fantasies! What are the desires and ideas you would like you and your partner to experiment with? Where are these wishes coming from? Are they connected to pornography? If you were to act them out, what effect would it have on your relationship? If you were to engage in those sex acts, would you be expressing your love, or would you only be using your partner?

---

[1]Stephen and Alex Kendrick, *The Love Dare*, p. 112. [2]Patrick Carnes, *Out of the Shadows: Understanding sexual addiction*, p. 30. [3]Patrick Carnes, *Out of the Shadows: Understanding sexual addiction*, pp. 29-30. [4]Patrick Carnes, *Out of the Shadows: Understanding sexual addiction*, pp. 6, 14. [5]Judith A. Reisman, 'The Psychopharmacology of Pictorial Pornography Restructuring Brain, Mind & Subverting Freedom of Speech', p. 21. *http://www.drjudithreisman.com* (6/8/2014). [6]It is important to note that the Bible doesn't limit sexuality to procreation, but embraces its role in pleasure and relationship enrichment. For example, the *Song of Songs*, which contains vivid descriptions of lovemaking, calls sexuality a flame that comes from God (Song of Songs 8:6). It is worth mentioning here that the biblical story from which the term *onanism* comes, which is often used for masturbation, is not about masturbation but about interrupted intercourse (*coitus interruptus*) (Genesis 38). [7]ICD-10, F65.2 [8]ICD-10, F65.3 [9]It is sobering to check your county's statistics on the issue. A global statistic: every year one million girls are sold as sex slaves, often

with the knowledge and assistance of their parents. [10]Carnes, *Out of the Shadows*, pp. 68-73. [11]Carnes, *Out of the Shadows*, pp. 66-67. [12]Carnes, *Out of the Shadows*, pp. 167-168. [13]Source: *https://saa-recovery.org/OurProgram/TheTwelveSteps* (date: 3/3/2017). [14]Kornelius Roth, *Sexsucht*, p. 101. [15]*www.shessomebodysdaughter.com/get-the-facts-about-pornography* (date: 19/11/2014). [16]A. Bridges, R. Wosnitzer, E. Sharrer, C. Sun & R. Liberman, 'Aggression and sexual behavior in best-selling pornography: A content analysis update'. *Violence Against Women*. Source: *http://journals.sagepub.com/doi/pdf/10.1177/1077801210382866*. [17]Victor B. Cline, *Pornography's Effects on Adults and Children* (New York: Morality in Media, 2001). Quoted: Robert W. Peters, Laura J. Lederer & Shane Kelly, 'The Slave and the Porn Star: Sexual Trafficking and Pornography', *Journal of Human Rights and Civil Society*, 2012/5, p. 10. [18]*https://www.shelleylubben.com*/stats (date: 19/11/2014). [19]Gottman & Silver, *What Makes Love Last?* p. 62.

Talk! Talk! Talk!

During my teenage years I went through several stages that were defined by a particular music band or a style of music. Like most teenagers, I had a metal era, a rap era, a rock era, a funk era and even a classical music era. Somewhere in the middle of my funk era the radios kept playing the song, *Let's talk about sex*, by the Salt-N-Pepa girl band. I remember that, due to my somewhat prudish environment, I was shocked that anyone could call on us to discuss sexuality this openly. But today I'm convinced that it is not only possible to discuss sexuality frankly – it is a must! Although, maybe not in the way the girls did on the radio.

The connection of talking about sex and sexual satisfaction

I have previously quoted the research of one of my university classmates, Ralf Näther. According to him, the highest sexual satisfaction is achieved by those couples who (1) have never experienced infidelity, (2) are having sex 2-3 times a week, and (3) are relaxed about their sexuality, discussing it freely and trying out new ways to enjoy it. In the opposite corner are the couples who (1) have experienced infidelity, (2) rarely have sex, and (3) are cautious and negative about sexual novelties and avoid talking about sex. This supports the conclusion that we need to discuss our sexual experiences, joys, wishes and fantasies – even our fears and pains – with our partners. The question is: how to start? I will try to provide help in order to start the discussion, but I am aware that there are couples who will need more assistance.

During couples therapy it often becomes clear that sex is a word that can evoke painful memories of quarrels, emotional eruptions and deep hurt. Men often become tense, their faces turn red and I can see that they are struggling as to whether they should speak up or not. Women often just sit with arms folded defensively, obviously uncomfortable discussing something that they would prefer to avoid. Their legs are often crossed and their bodies turned away from their partners, as if ready to make a quick departure if opportunity presents itself.

There is one more important issue here. Many consider openness to mean the openness of the relationship to the outside, but I mean openness *inside* the boundaries of the relationship. As Clinebell puts it: 'I'm all for an "open marriage" in terms of communication, equality, growth and outside friendship. But if "open" means sexual affairs, the results are usually not openness or growth – or really liberating sex!'[1]

In other words, we need to talk, and if we do not succeed we should ask for help, because once the relationship sours, talking about sex will do more to damage than to benefit.

The levels of intimate communication

Intimate communication in relationships is to be treasured. Everybody wants to have it, but for most people it has either broken down or reached a dead end. If you have read my book, *I Do – How to Build a Great Marriage*, or you have participated in my marriage enrichment seminar called Connect, then you are aware of the concept discussed next, and the onion-like layers that constitute intimate communication. Every layer is a step towards our innermost being, our core self, and the deeper we let others in, the more vulnerable we become. At the same time, however, this vulnerability is our opportunity for greater intimacy.

Level 5: Cliché level
At this level people do not disclose anything personal. Instead, they stick with clichés or hide behind questions. The typical questions of this level are: 'What's up?' 'How was your day?' and so on. Discussions are usually short, shallow and impersonal. Those who communicate primarily at this level in their marriage will soon find themselves frustrated, and feel that their relationship is empty and cold.

Level 4: The level of facts
Similarly, at this level we find those courteous discussions full of phrases behind which it is easy for people to hide their actual feelings and opinions. This type of conversation doesn't require a person to open up to others, because it consists of strictly factual and emotionally detached content. Many use this type of conversation to show that they are willing to engage. However, this level is not enough. Maybe the amount of communication is right, but there are problems with the quality, and in marriage the primary matter is not how long a conversation is, but how deep.

Level 3: The level of ideas and opinions
This is the first step in opening up as an individual. We begin to share some of our own views, a small part of ourselves. At this stage we usually watch the reactions of the partner

closely, and, if they respond positively to our cautious initial openness, we then move on to the next level.

Level 2: The level of emotion
Here we are getting to what makes us individual human beings. Our particular thoughts and emotions distinguish us from all other humans – they are unique to us. At this level deep, honest and open conversations evolve. At the end of this chapter I will help you articulate your emotions, for sometimes we are unable to put into words what is going on inside us, and because of this we are unable to communicate them to our partner.

Level 1: The level of intimate communication
Whoever opens up at this level risks vulnerability, due to the disclosure of what is in the deepest chambers of their being to the other person. Maybe the reason why the word *intimacy* is often used as a synonym for sex, and why it often refers to sexual closeness, is that intimacy means, in the psychological sense, the nakedness of the human soul. If it happens in a safe atmosphere, where mutual acceptance occurs, this level of communication becomes an inexhaustible resource for the marriage. Truly happy couples often meet each other at this level. The spiritual nakedness is naturally followed by a physical nakedness, and in this way we are able to experience the beauty of becoming one body in sex. This provides the possibility of experiencing fullness without feeling coercion or guilt or shame. This is what makes the couple's togetherness deep and exclusive, and this generates a sure protection against outer forces that may wish to intrude.

I have observed two points of communication impasse among couples I have worked with in counselling. The first happens when a couple get stuck in shallow communication and are unable to move to deeper levels. Such couples face two options: they either give up on having deeper intimacy and a sexual life, and function like flatmates (often bitter, disappointed and on the lookout for replacement activities); or they detach sexuality from communication. They don't talk about ideas and emotions, but have sex regularly. Interestingly, when this happens they tend to have the same attitude towards strangers as well, with whom they have no emotional attachment whatsoever. I have met men and women who are unable to share more than two or three meaningful and coherent sentences with each other, who often have sex with others outside the relationship.

The other communication logjam occurs when, without any foreplay, the partners pounce on each other and engage in very deep levels of sexual intimacy. One man contacted me because their intimacy didn't work any more, and they hadn't had sex for several months. He reported that when they had had a good sexual life, sex came unexpectedly and spontaneously. When I asked him to provide some examples of what he meant, he listed some very interesting situations. For example, he reported that once, while on the motorway, his wife started to stroke his thigh, while her eyes said that it was time to find a parking lot. Once, while he was hoovering, his wife jumped up from the couch, grabbed his penis and said: 'Stop hoovering and let's have sex!' Even though these stories may sound very passionate and exciting, it is very telling that this man had turned to me with an intimacy problem. In my experience the human being is unable to cope without a more gradual transition into intimacy. At the start of a relationship such impromptu sex can work for a while and can be exciting, especially for the man, but after a while it becomes unnatural and too forceful. This is why it is important to know how we get to the core of that 'onion': moving gradually from superficial clichés to a deep intimacy that encompasses our desires and dreams.

Four steps towards true understanding

If a couple are to communicate on the deeper levels, they have to find a way to communicate intimately. Many only speak, without giving attention to what the other one is telling them or what the other one needs. Like children playing in the same sandbox, one is pushing his little car, the other is playing with his toy soldiers and neither of them is paying attention to the other. The great Swiss child psychologist, Jean Piaget, called this phenomenon a 'collective monologue'. On many occasions adults, and even intimate partners, conduct such monologues as a poor substitute for real dialogue. An intimate discussion is an entry ticket into the inner world of our partner. A simple conversation that assures our spouse that we are listening, that we are really interested, so much so that we have turned towards him or her with warmth and acceptance, can help open up his or her heart.

Dr Gottman gives us a four-step guide on how to achieve this.[2]

Step 1. Articulate your feelings

It is very surprising to see how difficult people find it to articulate their feelings: especially men, who are usually used to arguing and finding solutions. Irrespective of gender differences, we tend to start sentences with 'YOU', which communicates feelings not directly, but indirectly. For example, when the wife says to her husband, 'You have once again left the plates on the table!' she actually means, 'I feel that my work is considered less important and less valuable compared to yours, and you do not value what I do for our family!' This second sentence is an 'I' sentence, and it is about the feelings that the person is experiencing. If we were to communicate this way in our everyday conversations we would experience the benefits, even if it may sound a bit artificial at first. The first step is to understand what our feelings are and then share them with our spouse. The following chart may be of help:

Positive feelings and moods	Negative feelings and moods
carefree, relaxed, satisfied, happy, enthusiastic, grateful, excited, amused, thrilled, upbeat, peaceful, playful, contented, relaxed, calm, satisfied, proud, determined, energetic, confident, strong, curious, passionate, sexy, funny, eager, relieved, well (whole), focused, loving, radiant, touched, lively, sensual, full of life, devoted, amazed, surprised, expectant, liberated, warm-hearted, understood, gentle, dashing, heroic, well-rested, fresh	resentful, helpless, bitter, gloomy, melancholic, ashamed, humiliated, frustrated, frightened, angry, aloof, silent, useless, shocked, alienated, confused, irritated, petulant, provoked, suspicious, scattered, fragmented, puzzled, unstable, apathetic, sceptical, unscrupulous, panicked, hysterical, isolated, overwhelmed, indifferent, insensitive, rigid, tense, nervous, falling apart, estranged, empty, exhausted, weak, aggressive

2. Ask open-ended questions!

Much is dependent on the use of questions in a conversation, so a good conservation partner will know how to ask questions. They will know the difference between *yes-no* and *open-ended questions* and how to use them the right way. It is easy to distinguish between the two types of question if you think of the answer. A *yes-no* question can be answered with a very short answer, usually with either 'yes' or 'no'. The open-ended questions require a longer answer with more explanation. Both have advantages and disadvantages, which need to be considered when you choose your questions.

Open-ended questions tend to calm the situation, and make the conversation deeper and more interesting with longer answers. The disadvantage is that, in some situations, they will produce long, shallow clichés. For example, if the question is, 'How was your day?' the husband might feel too tired to talk about all of his day, and will answer, 'Nothing interesting!' So the question requiring a shorter answer would have been more useful, like, 'How was the mood in the office?'

Yes-no questions have the advantage that they elicit exact answers with specific information. The disadvantage is that if there are too many of them, they will make the conversation boring, with lots of pauses. And that might make one feel like he or she is being interrogated.

3. Deepen your partner's expression
We can do a lot to make conservation deeper if we reflect the words of our partner. Your partner will feel that you are paying attention to what he or she is saying, and this will help them open up even more, thereby sharing more emotions. Here are a couple of examples:

Wife: 'Today I looked at our wedding pictures again. How young and how much in love we were!'
Husband: 'So, you had some nostalgic moments about that time when our lives had fewer responsibilities and we had more time for each other?'

Husband: 'It has been so long since we did something together, just the two of us, without the children.'
Wife: 'Would you like it if we organised some time alone, when we could listen only to each other and we wouldn't have to keep our eyes on the children?'

4. Express your sympathy!

The conversation may come to an end if one party doesn't pay attention or show sympathy, but rejects the speaker, or offers solutions. In an intimate conversation the point is not to solve the speaker's problem, but to make them feel how important they are, and that we take them and their emotions seriously. The person doesn't need to be afraid of anything, because there will be no rejection. A lot depends on the kind of short comments we make in these situations. We can use very brief comments to enhance the conversation, or we can shut the person up completely, putting them on the defensive. Once people feel they need to defend themselves, that signals the end of intimacy. The following will help to keep a conversation flowing and make it deeper:

- I can see that this is really hurting you.
- It hurts me, too, to hear what you are saying.
- No wonder you became angry.
- If someone said this to me, I would be hurt too.
- Oh, my dear, this must have been really bad for you.
- This situation would have tried my patience as well.
- I believe I know what you mean. Did you want to say something like this . . . ?
- What I really admire about you is that in this situation you . . .
- This sounds scary, but I wouldn't know what to do either.

Let's talk about sex – but how?

There are many reasons why someone avoids intimate subjects, one of the most obvious being that they have never learned how to discuss them. Some believe that if their partner really loves them, they should know what to do anyway. Why talk about it? But it is not right to think that. Just because we love someone, it doesn't mean we will be able to read their mind. Good sex does not happen automatically, and it takes a concerted effort to find each other's sexual frequency. What arouses the one might not be as pleasant to the other. It helps a lot if we can express what is good for us, and what is not.

Some choose to remain silent because they do not want to hurt the feelings of their spouse. However, not to tell the truth can also be hurtful. It is less hurtful to say - with love and kindness - what we would like to change.

It is also possible that someone may not be aware of their own feelings, thoughts and needs. What we ourselves cannot articulate will be difficult to communicate to others, even if we love them.

Whatever might be the reason for the discussion, before we start we should define what our purpose is for having it. If we know where we want to be, it will be easier to find the road there. We can have several goals:[3]

- To let the partner know what is important to me
- To discuss how to improve our sexual life
- To solve our differences in sexual appetite and interest
- To share fantasies
- To clarify misunderstandings
- To discuss vulnerabilities
- To share sexual wishes
- To express interest and affection
- To increase enjoyment
- To make sexuality more playful

Once you know what the goal of your discussion is, then start the discussion, following some guidelines:[4]

Make sure to start with a positive message! Sex is a very sensitive subject and it is important to talk about it in a relaxed, pleasant, tension-free atmosphere. It is very hard, if not impossible, to correct a harsh start and end up with a positive result. Gottman observed: 'When a discussion leads off like this – with criticism and/or sarcasm, a form of contempt – it has begun with a "harsh start-up". . . . The research shows that if your discussion starts with a harsh start, it will inevitably end on a negative note, even if there are a lot of attempts to "make [it] nice" in between. Statistics tell the story: 96 percent of the time you can predict the outcome of a conversation based on the *first three minutes* of the fifteen-minute interaction! A harsh start simply dooms you to failure.'[5]

Instead of criticising, say what you want to achieve! If there is a good atmosphere, you can start sharing what you want to do differently in your sexual life. Do not blame your partner! If you attack, your partner will automatically become defensive and it will end up in a fight. You should rather state your wishes calmly, because quiet openness is more likely to awaken the partner's sympathy. Make use of this power! Instead of saying: 'I do not appreciate it when you turn over and fall asleep after sex!' you should rather say: 'It is so good when, after sex, we hold each other in our arms and I can look into your eyes. This means so much to me and I would like it to happen more often.'

Be specific! Speak about what you want to do in specific terms! If you vent your frustration, it will not solve the problem. Make what you want, or what you want to change, known to your partner. It is a myth that, if your partner loves you, they will know even your secret desires. Simply say it! It is not enough to say: 'I do not want to have sex; I want to make love!' Tell your partner exactly what the difference between the two is, and what makes 'making love' more than 'having sex'. Instead of saying: 'Be more passionate!' say: 'I love it when you make sounds while making love, and when I feel from your gestures and breathing that what I'm doing feels pleasurable to you. It excites me when you are a bit more forceful and hold me tight!' Instead of saying: 'You should initiate love-making as well sometimes!' you should rather say: 'It feels good when you look at me during the day in that special way, and you ask me if we should go upstairs to the bedroom. I also like it when you grab me by surprise and I can see in your eyes that you want me. This gives me happiness and pleasure. I would like you to do this more often!'

Use I-messages that create the opportunity to be more specific and clearer about what is on your mind without attacking the other person. Instead of saying: 'I do not like it when you are impatient and to the point!' rather say: 'When you are aroused already, I may still need time to get in the mood. I would like to play a little bit longer. Wait for me and then we can pick up steam together. It would feel more as if you care for me and you really want to be with me.'

If things get tense, take a break! To open up in the area of sex makes one vulnerable, and it can really hurt if, during the heat of the discussion, something hurtful is said. Avoid this! Agree that if the discussion becomes too heated then you will do something different for a while, either together or separately. Do not get carried away because of bitterness or hurt and say things that will haunt you later. Use your words in a manner that you would like to hear them said to you. By the way, if things get out of hand on the positive side, take a break, and do something else. . . .

Emotions are not bad or good; they just are! We cannot direct them with our will, so we cannot argue with them either. If you feel something, then that is what you feel and it is the reality of the situation. It is also dangerous if someone wants to argue against the other's emotions, because it will make your partner close up next time, instead of opening up. And this is a marriage killer.

Do not be a mind-reader! However deeply we love each other, we have no access to each other's thoughts. Do not expect your partner to know what you want, so tell them, clearly and kindly, exactly what you have in mind. Similarly, make sure you are responding to what your partner has actually said, and not to what you believe your partner thinks. It means that if you are in the process of formulating an idea, you should grant your partner access to this process. Do not just confront him or her with the end product, but make your partner understand how you got there, because if your mate doesn't understand the process, it might anger him or her.

The past stays in the past! It is really hard to talk about sex if you carry deep hurts from the past – for example, if one of you was unfaithful. If this is the case, these issues should be processed first, for it is not fair to let past grievances intrude on the present where they can be used to exercise leverage on each other. If you have settled the issue, and if there was an apology and the granting of forgiveness (getting to phase three, as seen before), then the past should stay in the past. If you haven't settled the issue then you should do it urgently, because you cannot move on successfully until you have dealt with it. It causes a really bad feeling if someone feels his or her spouse abuses sex, using it as a tool to manipulate or even blackmail them.

Do not generalise! Due to the nature of sex all the little details matter, and our senses will be receptive even to small stimuli that we wouldn't have noticed otherwise. Be careful with how you word things! Avoid saying 'always' and 'never' and similar expressions. These expressions are capable of causing hurt that will be hard to heal. Not long ago, I had a revelation during a therapeutic session where the discussion was about the sexual satisfaction of the couple. The wife was complaining that in 80% of their sexual encounters it was only about satisfying her husband's needs, and that she rarely enjoyed it. As she uttered these words, I could see the husband sinking and sinking deeper into the couch until he was annihilated. In just under 30 seconds the wife had managed to throw him into an abyss. Sexual performance is used to measure manliness – the criterion being whether or not a man is able to arouse and pleasure a woman and make her happy. A few minutes later we were discussing orgasm, and the wife said that in 80 to 90% of their intercourse she had experienced orgasm. The husband's self-worth immediately started to recover, but her comments had raised a question: 80% of their sex was bad, but she was aroused to orgasm 80% of the time? Both bits of information couldn't be correct, could they? So, be careful about what you say and be very specific, otherwise it will really hurt.

Do not be discouraged if your partner is not in the same gear as you! If talking about sex is something new in your relationship, then be patient. Maybe your partner is still shy or embarrassed and will try to joke about or belittle aspects of the discussion. Maybe it is hard for him or her to be specific. This is a learning process, and you will have to go through it, both together and individually.

How to deal with secrets in the marriage?
Secrets are very dangerous. In the beginning they may look like innocent little lies and they even lend a special kind of excitement to the relationship. In the long run, however, they tend to alienate the partners. What may, at first, seem to be just a bit of withheld information (a secret) can soon be seen as an attempt to cover up and deceive (a lie). In the end, the partner has to work hard to keep the secret and it will inevitably lead to a long chain of problems.

As we have already concluded, the marriage is a relationship where the married partners have 'arrived'. From the 'searching' phase they have entered into the 'being found' state, where they take off their 'armour'. It means they form an intimate community in which there is trust. Patton and Childs say that intimacy is a desire to show ourselves as we are, risking even shame by giving I-messages and tuning in to the needs of the other party, instead of just searching for our own fulfilment.[6] In life there are so many masks we can wear, but in marriage we can be ourselves, in a safe environment, taking off our masks and lowering our defences to declare: 'This is who I am; this is my authentic self!' If we truly want an intimate, honest and deep relationship, we have to live without secrets. The information that we might be tempted to withhold from our spouse can be grouped into three subgroups.

1. Secrets
I would put into this category all the information that someone withholds from their spouse on purpose because they are afraid of the consequences, or of losing some personal advantage. It might be an affair the husband has on the go with his secretary, which he doesn't want his wife to know about, but it could also be a sickness that the bride

hasn't shared with the groom because she is afraid he will not marry her if she does. (I once encountered a case where the whole family of the groom conspired to hide his serious psychotic problem from the bride in order to rid themselves of any responsibility for him.) It could also be a serious addiction that is not shared honestly, or even an unpleasant episode from the past, like the man who only told his bride that he was divorced a few days before the wedding. She came from a conservative family and this news was devastating to her.

There is one common element in all of these stories: one party concealed information that the other one had the right to know. The information was important and should have been shared, but the person chose to hide it because of the fear that it might cause negative consequences or deprive them of a benefit.

2. Surprises

We could consider surprises as secrets too, because they also involve one party withholding information from the other. However, withholding this information is not to the detriment of the partner, but for their benefit. Here the intention is to keep something secret so that at the right time it will cause even greater joy. Think of a trip that you prepare for in secret; or a gift that you kept hidden for a memorable occasion.

A German couple come to mind, one with whom we have been friends for a long time. The husband noticed how much his wife liked a certain decoration in the Christmas window of a shop. It consisted of candles on a wooden structure that turned the sails of a mill. When he saw how much she liked the mill, he decided to build one for her, even though it involved several hundred parts. He carefully researched how to make one, and, being a very good handyman, he set to work in his garage to create it. The result was so good that his wife couldn't believe that he had made it when he gave it to her on Christmas Eve. Suddenly it became clear why her husband had spent so much extra time working in his garage every afternoon.

I have to admit that I couldn't do something like that. Once I tried to buy Dora's Christmas present in September. She is a passionate photographer and I decided to buy a camera that she would really like in every detail. I did extensive research into the various models on the internet, just to make sure I would be buying the best for her, but, because I had to do this all in secret, I started to feel bad. I felt that I was hiding a significant part of my life from my wife, whom I really love, and who is very close to me. After a while I felt so uncomfortable that I couldn't keep my secret any more. I confessed to Dora and we made the decision of what camera to buy together.

I don't believe that keeping something intended to be a surprise secret is essentially wrong, but whoever decides to do so must take care not to make the partner insecure and suspicious in the process. After all, you don't want your partner thinking, 'If he was able to make this happen in secret, without me noticing anything, then what would he do if he got to know someone pretty . . . ?' And this is the point where it gets slippery. . . .

3. Private area
There are other issues that we may not want to share with our spouse because they are part of our most private inner world. These are not things that influence our relationship; they don't distract us from our responsibilities; and are in no way harmful to our partner. This might initially sound strange, giving the impression that our partner need not be

party to our most innate (originating in the mind) world. I am not suggesting that. So let me illustrate it with two circles that overlap 90%. In a similar way, we each share most of our life with each other, but there remains a tiny section that only we have access to. It may involve work-related information, especially if we are bound by privacy or confidentiality agreements, or even dreams, fantasies and fleeting thoughts that we haven't sought or cultivated – they have just come and left as quickly. If we were to disclose these thoughts to each other, although we might forget them, they might easily lodge themselves in our spouse's mind or vice versa.

Warning! This small, private space that you reserve for yourself cannot be used to store the details of a secret affair, or of any other things that happened in the past that can impact your relationship in the present. The only things that can be kept here are those that could have happened, but didn't. No one could understand this situation better than Udo Jürgens, the German singer. In one of his songs[7] he gives us a glimpse of an evening with a family through the eyes of the father. After supper, the husband tells his wife that he is going out to buy some cigarettes at the little corner shop. The wife suggests that he take his keys as she is going to bathe the baby. As the husband closes the door and goes outside via the staircase, he suddenly wonders what it would be like if he were to leave now for good, and go on to see the wider world. The refrain of the song is:

I've never been to New York, I've never been to Hawaii
Never walked through San Francisco in a pair of torn jeans
I've never been to New York, I've never been really free
Just be crazy for once and break the chains.[8]

As he steps out of the house into the street he realises that he has all that he needs: passport, credit card and cash, and maybe there is a flight tonight. His desire keeps growing: just to be filled, once again, by dreams; to once more break out of his confined life. Then he puts the cigarettes into his pocket and his legs start to take him home, back into the staircase smelling of floor polish and lit by neon lights. His wife asks him where he has been that it took him so long, because it is time for the evening TV contest to start. She then asks him: 'Has something happened?'

He answers: 'No, what should have happened?' And again, in his mind, the fading melody of the refrain is repeated:
I've never been to New York, I've never been to Hawaii
Never walked through San Francisco in a pair of torn jeans
I've never been to New York, I've never been really free
Just be crazy for once and break the chains.

Yes, these are ideas that have probably popped up in every husband's mind. 'What if . . . ?' 'If only there could be just one more time . . .' 'How would my life have been if I had . . . ?' 'What if I would just simply . . . right now?' These thoughts generally leave as fast as they come, and we would not be doing our partners a favour to expose them to every idea that popped into our minds.

In another song[9] Jürgens looks out of the window of a plane, and sees the lights of a town below. A woman he never met before must live there. Maybe she is the one he has been looking for all the time. Maybe she is awake, reading a book. Maybe she is awake and, looking into the sky, she sees the plane passing by. And here comes the refrain:
The woman I never met: I know she exists.
If we'd met we would have loved each other for ever.
The woman I never met: it looks so far away, yet so close.
Maybe this is just a memory of something that never happened.

The plane lands; the man goes to the hotel and can see the thousand windows from close by. Some still show light. And maybe he has already passed the window of the woman he never met, and missed his last chance to meet her.

If a man were to cherish a thought like this long enough, then his searching eyes would see in every woman one he 'never met'. And this might result in a situation that would be dangerous for his marriage. An idea flaring up in our thoughts is innocent, not dangerous. But once we start to feed it and make a script out of it, then the emergency lights should start to flash. The 'memories' of events that never happened should never become the prophecies of events to come!

In an ideal world – a state of Paradise – to be naked without any cover and mask, just like Adam and Eve, is nothing to be ashamed of; there is nothing to hide. However, our world is not perfect and innocent any more, and neither are we. So spare your spouse your random thoughts or fleeting dreams.

I agree with Arnold Lazarus, who assigns the letters of the alphabet to the full spectrum of honesty.[10] He says that if honesty ranges from A to Z, then marital transparency ranges from A to V. I would place these random thoughts and fleeting dreams into the W, X, Y and Z part of his honesty spectrum. They are not the result of premeditation or malice and pose no direct threat to the relationship. However, I do not agree with him that infidelity belongs to the W-to-Z category, that private area that no one should be privy to. By agreeing with that, I would have to accept that sexuality can exist outside of a relationship and that sexual impulses outside the relationship do not have any effect on it, which is simply not the case. Just as with our gender, our sexuality is part of our identity and cannot be separated from our relationship identity, or from our feeling of security and our jointly forged WE identity. Infidelity undermines all of these at the deepest level.

Summary

It is vitally important to talk about sex in a relationship, and to experience its deep intimacy often. When talking about sex, it is important to be accurate and positive in order not to offend our partner. If a person shuts the partner out from important parts of his or her life and keeps secrets, it will undermine the relationship. However, it is not advisable to share all our stray thoughts, for, although they may be unimportant, they may be misunderstood and injure the relationship. Do not be honest from A to Z – it is enough to talk openly about things in the A to V category.

What this all means for the three types of marriage I presented you with in the beginning of chapter 2, is summarised in the following table.

The three types of marriage and sex talk

Superficial	Functional	Deep
The couple's relationship culture doesn't include how to share their thoughts about sexuality. Most probably they haven't seen any authentic patterns, and as adults they haven't learned any yet. Even if they talk about it, they do so in a vulgar and superficial manner. If something	This couple haven't talked much about sex, and whenever they do they end up feeling uneasy. Many are even afraid of the word 'sex', so they rather avoid the topic altogether. Many of them have had a conservative and prudish upbringing. Their motto is: 'It is inappropriate to talk about certain topics,	The couple are aware of the importance of talking about sex and make efforts to do so, even though they may have had negative experiences in the past. They respect each other's feelings, use 'I-messages', and emphasise their needs and wishes instead of telling each other off. They use a rich vocabulary to express

| is not exciting enough for them, they demand a change rather than stating their emotions and needs. Their motto is: 'Everyone needs to make love, but not to talk about it.' | and sex is one of them.' Their conversation rarely goes deeper than the level of facts and opinions. | their emotions. They often meet on the deepest levels. |

Exercises

1. Expressing your emotions directly

This exercise will help you to express your emotions directly. In the first column you will find examples of how emotions may be expressed indirectly (YOU-messages). Read the sentence and find the emotion expressed in the sentence. After finding it, rewrite the sentence so that it will directly communicate the emotion you have experienced (an I-message).

Indirect message (YOU-message)	Emotion in the sentence	Direct message (I-message)
It was really unkind of you to pull your face away when I wanted to kiss you.	Feeling rejected	I felt rejected when you pulled away your face. It felt really bad.
You are only affectionate if you want something from me.		
You are only interested in your own satisfaction.		
I saw how you were staring at her!		
You haven't even looked at me for a week!		

Do you always have to text during supper?		
Do you think that it is OK, after not seeing each other for the whole day, that in the evening we jump straight into bed?		
Be a little bit more romantic!		
That is a very sensitive body part. It was good, but you shouldn't be pulling it as if to tear it off.		
Do you always have to do it the same way? Can't you be a little bit more spontaneous?		
You just lie here like a piece of wood!		

2. Sentences that help establish an intimate conversation

Finish these sentences, then find a way to share them with your partner! It would be good if your partner could also finish the sentences so that you can share them with each other.

You can strongly affect me when . . .

You do best when . . .

I feel that you really want me when . . .

Your sexiest body part is . . . because . . .

The part of my body I love the most is . . . because . . .

It is most exciting when . . .

During love-making I like to see that . . .

One of my most exciting sexual fantasies is that . . .

One of our best experiences of sex was when . . .

I believe I can arouse you the most when . . .

3. 'Darling, we should talk!'
What is the most important topic that you need to discuss with your spouse, but about which it is difficult for you to start the conversation? Define the topic and sketch a plan of the conversation. Also write down what you want to avoid, so as not to get into an impasse during the conversation.

The subject to discuss:

The steps in the conversation:

Possible traps and pitfalls:

4. From A to V
This is an exercise that you have to do when circumstances are calm and you are alone! If you both read this book, use separate sheets of paper and, if you feel it necessary, tear them up afterwards. 'If honesty ranges from A to Z, then desired marital transparency ranges from A to V.'

What is in A to Z in your life?

What could endanger your faithfulness towards your spouse?

Do you want to share this with your spouse? If yes, what is your plan?

[1]Clinebell, Howard J., *Growth Counseling for Marriage Enrichment*, p. 24. [2]John Gottman and Nan Silver, *What Makes Love Last?* pp. 93-99. [3]Michele Weiner Davis, *The Sex-Starved Marriage*, p. 187. [4]Michele Weiner Davis, *The Sex-Starved Marriage*, pp. 187-197. [5]John Gottman and Nan Silver, *The Seven Principles of Making Marriage Work*, p. 27. [6]John Patton and Brian H. Childs, *Generationsübergreifende Ehe- und Familienseelsorge*, p. 120. [7]Udo Jürgens: *Ich war noch niemals in New York*. [8]http://www.oktoberfest-songs.com/ich-war-noch-niemals-in-new-york-lyrics.html [9]Udo Jürgens: *Die Frau die ich nie traf*. [10]Arnold Lazarus, *Marital Myths Revisited: A Fresh Look at Two Dozen Mistaken Beliefs About Marriage*.

10 They should know better: **doctors, psychologists, teachers, lawyers and priests**

A couple in their fifties who lived far away once came to me for help. The man was a medical doctor, and it was important for him to confide in a therapist who had no prior knowledge of him or any of his colleagues. His wife worked in a bank. The problem they wanted help for was a very current one. The husband was involved in an affair that he wanted to end, but the woman he was involved with had threatened to commit suicide if he did. The deeper we dug, the more I realised that there was a pattern going back for years, even decades, that this man was persistently following. After five sessions I concluded that he was a sexual predator who abused the trust of the doctor-patient relationship to start sexual relations with his patients by using the intimate nature of his treatments as a launchpad.

His position of authority, his social status and the patient's confusion may all have contributed to the start of these relationships. After practising this 'second profession' for many years, it threatened to suck him into a vortex that would destroy all he had: marriage, family, career, reputation, wealth, his whole existence, simply everything.

A young woman attending an institution of higher education once told me that she had had to start learning a musical instrument for her studies. Her friends suggested that the guitar would be the easiest instrument to learn, so she contacted a guitar teacher. The first lesson involved learning the correct breathing technique, and they started with breathing exercises. From the second class onwards, the girl had to do the exercises while the teacher stood behind her and put his hand on her stomach just to check if she was doing the exercises correctly. Sometimes his hands would 'accidentally' slide up to her breasts and she would feel his erect penis touching her buttocks.

A woman in her sixties had a similar experience. She had her first sexual encounter at the age of fourteen with her piano teacher. She and her female friend attended his lessons for years, and after some of these sessions they would go to his flat to 'relax'. During these visits this single man involved the girls in group sex with him, in such a way that it appeared as if they had forced themselves on him and that he had reluctantly accepted their advances.

The case that shocked me the most, however, was of a wife and mother in her thirties who sobbingly told me that her father would get into bed beside her and masturbate while touching her. Later, in her teenage years, her uncle forced himself on her. Then finally, when he was taking her home after a Bible class, her pastor grabbed her hand and stuffed it into his underpants.

What is the common element in these stories? That men in positions of trust, be they doctors, teachers, lawyers or priests, who are valued and respected figures in society, have abused their positions. They have taken advantage of their social and professional standing and the trust invested in them to exploit women who were in vulnerable situations. Instead of helping them professionally they intentionally guided these women into sexual relationships in which they became abused victims. These men are what I call top sexual predators, who don't just make a mistake or display bad judgement, or forget to guard their boundaries. They systematically and intentionally eroticise such relationships, and from the outset they begin manipulating their victims into a sexual relationship.

I must also say that there are incidents where the roles are reversed. For example, I heard about a female teacher who enticed her students to satisfy her sexual needs in exchange for better grades; and, although this may be less common, it still causes similar traumatic damage. In the vast majority of cases the perpetrators are men, and this is supported by several studies that have produced reliable data on the subject. My own shocking findings have prompted me to pay more attention to the issue and I feel as if my mission is to raise awareness about this seldom-discussed topic, thereby helping to reduce the number of people who become traumatised in this way. The person who has made a real contribution through his research into this subject is Peter Rutter, who summarised his findings in his book, *Sex in the Forbidden Zone*, which is based on his interviews with several hundred women. The stories form a pattern that identifies the women who are likely to be victimised, and the men who are likely to become sexual predators, and how the process develops from an innocent doctor-patient relationship to sexual exploitation.

Let me start with what the author considers as sex in the forbidden zone: 'My position is that any sexual behaviour by a man in power within what I define as the forbidden zone is inherently exploitative of a woman's trust. Because he is the keeper of that trust, it is the man's responsibility, no matter what the level of provocation of apparent consent by the woman, to ensure that sexual behaviour does not take place.

... Sex in the forbidden zone [includes all] sexual behaviour between a man and a woman who have a professional relationship based on trust, specifically when the man is the woman's doctor, psychotherapist, pastor, lawyer, teacher or workplace mentor.'[1]

As you can see from his list, these professional relationships may be of different types, and they may become erotic in different ways, but the end results don't differ. The common basic elements expected from the role of a doctor, of a psychologist or of a pastor are trust and intimate privacy. Women often share with these professionals secrets that they don't share with anyone else, not even with their spouses. These professionals are usually very empathetic, accepting individuals who create a warm atmosphere in which the women relax and can shed their 'armour'. Many women say that they haven't received so much attention, even from their husbands or fathers over several years, as what they receive in just an hour from these professionals. The lawyers are less trained in handling emotions, but they have real power, and the client is often in a dependent position. A workplace mentor-intern or a school teacher-student relationship may also make one obliged and thankful to the mentor/teacher who has helped her to build up her career and connected her with influential people. The man then uses this obligation to manipulate the woman into a sexual relationship.

Rutter emphasises that in these boundary violations it is not simply fantasy that drives the events, but specific, pre-planned and executed acts. Much can happen in the mind, but there is a big difference between the thoughts and the deeds. Rutter is very honest when he writes about his own experiences from his own medical praxis: 'If we have been working together for some time, a familiarity and trust develops between us that starts to erode the boundaries of seemingly impersonal professional relationships. Whether they say so openly or not, these women often convey their feeling that we are treating them far better than they ever dreamed a man could. As a result, we may find ourselves experiencing a closeness, a comfort, a sense of completeness. . . .'[2]

Is there anything these victimised women have in common? The answer he gained from his research is a resounding 'yes'. There are a few female personality types that are more prone to exploitation than others, and who are intentionally targeted by these predators. Their common characteristics are:

- **Childhood sexual or psychological abuse.** The women who were sexually abused as little girls tend to develop behavioural patterns that drive them, time and time again, into similar situations.
- **Childhood experience of loneliness and isolation.** The unmet needs for respect, attention and equality can drive women to a point where they will allow the exploitation as a trade-off for these 'treasures'.
- **Exploited compassion.** This occurs where the victim has had to play the role of provider during childhood; has been cheated on as a wife; or has had to be the emotional resource 'bin' for others. It raises the risk of emotional exploitation if the woman has had to give a disproportionate amount of empathy and help to others without receiving much in return.
- **Devalued potential.** This arises in situations where the victim is repeatedly referred to as 'only a housewife', 'only a mother', or 'only a daughter'. If a woman is only valued by the important men in her life because of her ability to keep a household, and suddenly a helping professional shows her other areas in which she excels or has potential,

in this new-found freedom she may easily become vulnerable to her 'deliverer'.

What is the common characteristic across these types? Throughout life all of them have been made to believe that they are not valuable and loveable just as they are, but only if they perform to the expectations of others. If they want to have the respect and praise of a man, then their easiest way is to direct erotic signals towards him. The saddest part of the story is that they are not even aware of it.

How does this affect the helping professional? The man recognises the signals, and, totally misunderstanding the situation, he believes they are directed towards him personally – that it is a response to his manhood, his radiant personality and his attractiveness. The truth is that this type of communication is not flattering to his ego at all, but occurs simply because the woman doesn't know how to share her feelings in a healthy way. She has been conditioned to respond this way. If the helper doesn't realise this, he will join the line of men who have previously exploited her trust and just further confirm the status from which she seeks to escape. This will simply deepen the problem she seeks healing from. This is a tragic process, about which Rutter justly observes: 'As a symbol, however, the lack of childbearing after the injury of forbidden-zone sex suggests that the damage it creates goes to the very core of feminine existence, in much the same way as do the wounds of rape and incest.'[3] This fact should be taught to every person who is going to work as a helping professional. If a man engages in such forbidden-zone sex, he is establishing a sexual relationship with the woman such that, even if she started it, or gave her consent, the psychological trauma to her will be equivalent to rape!

How can we recognise the men in whom there is a dormant sexual predator only waiting for the opportune moment and the right prey? Well, there are no clues. I could compare the situation to one episode of the *Addams Family* show, where there is a masquerade party and a little girl turns up in her ordinary clothing. The others start to make fun of her, asking: 'You're not dressed in any disguise?' But she responds with: 'Yes, I am. I'm a serial killer and look just like anybody else.' This is how sexual predators dress. They look just like any other normal person. Rutter had the following to say about this: 'I also found that the men who have sex with their female patients, clients, parishioners, students, and protégées are not the obviously disturbed men showing up in the headlines. Instead, they are accomplished professionals, admired community leaders, and respectable family men whose integrity we tend to take for granted.'[4]

It is important to say that most doctors, psychologists, teachers, lawyers and pastors do their job according to strict ethical rules. They would never do anything like that, and are shocked and ashamed when they find out that a colleague has behaved disgracefully. Unfortunately, there are some professionals we should avoid, and for this reason it is important for potential victims to know the signs that indicate that such a situation is developing and when to get out of it. What are these telltale signs? Rutter has identified these in his research and describes the stages the predator uses to groom the victims for a sexual relationship.

- **He redefines the professional relationship as a sexual relationship.** The helping relationship is very stable at this point, and the trust is established. This firm foundation will then be used to try to redefine the relationship by testing the woman. For example, he will use ambiguous sentences and watch the woman's reactions. Maybe he will accidentally touch the woman inappropriately or in indecent places and wait to see if he is rejected or welcomed. Acceptance of the situation will be considered a licence to move on.

- **The man fantasises in the presence of the woman.** After the first tests, the predator starts to talk to the woman about his fantasies about her. First these are indirect and gentle attempts, often in the guise of professional counsel: 'If I were your husband, I wouldn't reject your initiations. I would be happy that such a beautiful woman desires me and wants to make love to me.'
- **The woman appears in the erotic fantasies of the man in her absence and the fantasy starts to exert a big influence.** This is the point the woman doesn't see. At this point the man starts to think of the woman as a woman and not as a 'case', and takes 'her' into his bedroom. In his head there are several further events and steps imagined and planned; those ideas have been vague, and only fleeting flashes are noticed in the office. We have already established this concerning our hormones: that an attachment can be formed with a person, an image or a scene if an orgasm is experienced while the thing is present. During masturbation the man starts to attach to the woman and is waiting excitedly for the next meeting, and starts planning the next steps.
- **They have a conversation about the woman's sexual experiences during counselling.** His intention may be dubious and difficult to prove, as talking about sexuality is often part of such therapy. The well-intentioned helper will mostly discuss the thoughts and feelings that the client experiences during sex and will be less curious about the technical details. If the professional wants to

know too many details, especially very intimate physical ones, this should cause caution and suspicion. Maybe he is only gathering sexual user data from her for his own fantasies.

- **He reduces the physical space and looks for a reaction.** Under the guise of help and trust, the man starts to draw physically closer to the woman. As the woman talks about hurtful experiences the man tries to comfort her by touching her or hugging her. It is important to know that you do not have to accept this kind of approach just because the person is your helper. Do not tolerate anything that you feel is inappropriate! To engage in touching between the helper and the client, other than the customary handshake, is unprofessional and unacceptable.

- **He starts to plan the specific steps and details of the seduction.** If the woman is receptive of these initial approaches the predator experiences acceptance and he will feel empowered to continue. He will begin flirting openly and touching without inhibition, even if there is no need to comfort. Already several boundaries have been violated, which will have reduced the physical gap between them.

- **He will contemplate practical considerations and conduct a risk evaluation.** This is also a step that is played out in the head of the man, hidden from the woman. The predator will consider the situation based on several evaluation factors and will evaluate the possible scenarios. *'What will happen if this is done? Is it safe? What are the risks? How can I deny it if it becomes public? What if the woman turns me down? What are the potential financial costs? What is the risk for my professional reputation? Would my family forgive me?'* At this point the concerns are not moral, but strategic. It is not a question of whether or not he is doing the right thing, but of whether or not he can get away with it.

- **He changes the nature of the meetings.** After surveying the risks, the man takes action. The first step is to change the setting. Maybe he will change the woman's session times to the evening, when no one is around; or he will offer to take her home. You would be surprised how many times I have heard that such boundary violations happened in a car – it seems that cars are highly erotic zones. Maybe he will invite her for dinner, or to his own flat.
- **The relationship turns openly erotic.** By now 'What if we . . . ?' sentences are used, with the goal that the man should be encouraged by the woman. He doesn't want to appear to be forcing things, as it is vital for his strategy that the woman should agree to the affair. He makes numerous promises. He confesses his love to her, talks about his bad marriage, and tells her that he is only together with his wife for the sake of the children. He tells her that he would be willing to leave his wife for a woman like her, and that she would be appreciated and loved by him. This is all very appealing for the woman who has been deprived of her self-worth.
- **The sexual act is performed.** The man will now turn into reality all that he has dreamed of – what he has toyed with in his mind countless times. He is following a strict script, and he knows every detail from his fantasies. The woman usually doesn't experience an orgasm, probably because she senses that the man is only using her. After sex she will feel dirty and humiliated, but she clears the man of any wrongdoing because he wasn't forceful. The woman feels like an accomplice in the whole story; she

feels ashamed and will not talk about what happened, and she rarely makes a complaint. As far as the predator is concerned – he already has his next victim in mind!

Who is to blame? Rutter believes the answer is obvious. This wasn't a mere coincidental cluster of events, but the result of a well-planned and executed strategy. Maybe he loses control at some point, but until then he makes many internal choices. In most such cases, these are intentional, manipulative and premeditated acts in which ethical and professional borders are willingly violated.

If you have experienced anything of the above, you should find the emergency exit fast. But it is important that you do not stop looking for help. You might have been unlucky enough to find an unethical helper, whose conduct is unprofessional and insincere, but the vast majority of professionals are **not like this!** If you have experienced something like this, then you should tell it to the next helper you contact. It is important to process this load of emotional trauma as well.

And what can an ethical helper do to avoid violating his professional boundaries?

Several points could be listed here from different sources, but I'm content with the following suggestions:
- Be in love with your spouse.
- Be aware of your vulnerability.
- Be perceptive.
- Be accountable.
- Be cautious of sexual counselling.
- Be ready to run.
- Be spiritually strong.

The professionals who faithfully follow this advice are unlikely to ruin their career, or the lives of those they serve.

[1]Rutter, *Sex in the Forbidden Zone,* pp. 23-24. [2]Rutter, *Sex in the Forbidden Zone,* p. 8.
[3]Rutter, *Sex in the Forbidden Zone,* p. 104. [4]Rutter, *Sex in the Forbidden Zone,* p. 2.

Epilogue

And now, on a personal note, let me end where I began this journey, with that timeless wisdom: 'So let the one who thinks he is standing be careful that he does not fall' (1 Corinthians 10:12, NET).

I sincerely hope that through the pages of this book I have managed to give you an appreciation of the importance, beauty and potential of a healthy marriage. At the same time, I trust that you are also more aware of the dangers that can threaten our marriages: those things that so easily derail our relationships, or send us down blind alleys from which retreat is difficult.

Now, at this point, as our journey closes, I trust that you will be able to echo this simple pledge with me:

'I am married, which means that I have narrowed my perception of intimacy to accept only the signals and responses of one person. I want to be a good man/woman for that person, and that person only. I have intentionally chosen her/him and don't want to spend the rest of my life looking for closeness and intimacy in the company of others. In fact, I have no desire or intention to squander the gift of my sexuality on anyone else.

'I will resolutely protect our relationship against all

intruders, taking special care to guard its boundaries in all circumstances. I will take responsibility for my words and actions. I will avoid ambiguous language that may encourage flirtation of any kind, and will make it clear to all that I love my spouse, and that I am not available for a relationship with anyone else.

'I intend to use every possible tool, and all the sound advice that is available, to improve our relationship and help our marriage achieve its fullest potential. To this end, I will consider every penny and every minute spent on improving our marriage to be a prime investment in the most important venture of my life.

'I will be proud of the strengths of our relationship, while working tirelessly to improve those areas that still require growth. I intend to transform our relational stumbling blocks into stable stepping stones, so that our children will have a good example to follow as they begin their own experience with intimacy.'

If you can repeat this little pledge without reservation, then this book has met its goals. Thank you for joining me on this journey! I wish you a happy, successful and exclusive marriage!

With warm regards,
Dr Gábor Mihalec

Selected bibliography

Almási, Kitti. *Hűtlenség . . . és ami mögötte van.* Budapest: Kulcslyuk, 2012.

Atkinson, Rita L. et al. (ed.). *Hilgard's Introduction to Psychology.* Fort Worth: Harcourt Brace College Publishers, 1996.

Bochmann, Andreas. *Praxisbuch Ehevorbereitung: Anregungen für Seelsorger und Berater.* Giessen, Basel: Brunnen, 2004.

Bochmann, Andreas; Näther, Ralf. *Sexualität bei Christen: Wie Christen ihre Sexualität leben und was sie dabei beeinflusst.* Giessen: Brunnen, 2002.

Bochmann, Andreas; van Treeck, Klaus-Jürgen (eds.). *Ehescheidung und Wiederheirat: Ein Pastoral-Theologisches Symposium.* Friedensau: Theologische Hochschule Friedensau, 2000.

Carnes, Patrick. *Out of the Shadows: Understanding Sexual Addiction.* Hazelden: Center City, 2001. Third edition.

Cline, Victor B. *Pornography's Effects on Adults and Children.* New York, New York: Morality in Media, 2001.

Clinebell, Howard J. *Growth Counseling for Marriage Enrichment.* Philadelphia: Fortress, 1982.

Cloud, Henry; Townsend, John. *Boundaries in Marriage.* Grand Rapids, Michigan: Zondervan, 1999.

Cloud, Henry; Townsend, John; Carden, Dave; Henslin, Earl. *Unlocking Your Family Patterns.* Chicago: Moody Publishers, 2011.

Craig, Bryan. *Searching for Intimacy in Marriage.* Silver Spring, Maryland:

General Conference Ministerial Association of Seventh-day Adventists, 2004.

Davis, Michele Weiner. *Divorce Busting: A Revolutionary and Rapid Program for Staying Together.* New York, New York: Simon & Schuster, 1992.

Davis, Michele Weiner. *The Sex-Starved Marriage. Boosting Your Marriage Libido: A Couple's Guide.* New York, New York: Simon & Schuster, 2003.

De Shazer, Steve. *Clues: Investigating Solutions in Brief Therapy.* New York, New York: W. W. Norton, 1988.

Dillow, Linda; Pintus, Lorraine. *Intimate Issues: Twenty-One Questions Christian Women Ask About Sex.* Colorado Springs, Colorado: Waterbrook Press, 1999.

Dobson, James. *Love Must Be Tough.* Nashville, Tennessee: Thomas Nelson, 1996.

Fowers, Blaine J.; Montel, Kelly H.; Olson, David H. 'Predicting Marital Success for Premarital Couple Types Based on PREPARE.' *Journal of Marital & Family Therapy,* 1996/22/1, pp. 103-119.

Gennep, Arnold van. *Übergangsriten (Les rites de passage).* Frankfurt/Main: Campus, 2005. Third edition.

Giubilini, Alberto; Minerva, Francesca. 'After-birth abortion: why should the baby live?' *Journal of Medical Ethics,* 2013/39/5, pp. 261-263.

Goleman, Daniel. *Emotional Intelligence: Why It Can Matter More than IQ.* New York, New York: Bantam, 1997.

Gottman, John M.; Silver, Nan. *What Makes Love Last? How to Build Trust and Avoid Betrayal.* New York, New York: Simon & Schuster, 2012.

Gottman, John M. *Why Marriages Succeed or Fail . . . And How You Can Make Yours Last.* New York, New York: Simon & Schuster, 1994.

Gottman, John M.; DeClaire, Joan. *The Relationship Cure: A 5-Step Guide to Strengthening Your Marriage, Family, and Friendships.* New York, New York: Three Rivers Press, 2001.

Gottman, John M.; Gottman, Julie Schwartz. *And Baby Makes Three: The Six-Step Plan for Preserving Marital Intimacy and Rekindling Romance After Baby Arrives.* New York, New York: Crown, 2007.

Gottman, John M.; Silver, Nan. *The Seven Principles for Making Marriage*

Work. New York, New York: Three Rivers Press, 2000.

Jellouschek, Hans. *Warum hast du mir das angetan? Untreue als Chance.* München: Piper, 2010. Tenth edition.

Kendrick, Stephen; Kendrick, Alex. *The Love Dare.* Nashville, Tennessee: B & H Publishing, 2008.

Lazarus, Arnold. *Marital Myths Revisited: A Fresh Look at Two Dozen Mistaken Beliefs About Marriage.* Atascadero, California: Impact Publishers, 2001.

Mace, David R. *Close Companions: The Marriage Enrichment Handbook.* New York, New York: Continuum, 1984.

Mace, David; Mace, Vera. *Love & Anger in Marriage: How to Manage Your Conflicts.* Basingstoke: Pickering & Inglis, 1983.

McIlhaney, Joe S.; McKissik Bush, Freda. *Hooked: New Science on How Casual Sex Is Affecting Our Children.* Chicago: Northfield, 2008.

Mihalec, Gábor. *A lelkigondozás és a pszichoterápia határkérdései a házassággondozásban. PhD doktori értekezés.* Budapest: Károli Gáspár Református Egyetem, 2013.

Mihalec, Gábor. *Ketten együtt, magabiztosan: Párkapcsolat-építő kommunikáció.* Budapest: Kulcslyuk, 2013.

Mihalec, Gábor. *I Do: How to Build a Great Marriage.* Hagerstown, Maryland: Review & Herald, 2014.

Morgenthaler, Christoph. *Systemische Seelsorge: Impulse der Familien- und Systemtherapie für die kirchliche Praxis.* Stuttgart: Kohlhammer, 2005. Fourth edition.

Norval, Glenn; Marquardt, Elizabeth. *Hooking Up, Hanging Out, and Hoping for Mr Right. College Women on Dating and Mating Today.* Washington DC: Institute for American Values, 2002.

Olson, David H.; Olson-Sigg, Amy; Larson, Peter J. *The Couple Checkup.* Nashville: Thomas Nelson, 2008.

Olson, David H.; DeFrain, John. *Marriages & Families: Intimacy, Diversity, and Strengths.* New York, New York: McGraw-Hill, 2006. Fifth edition.

Olson, David H.; Olson, Amy K. *Empowering Couples: Building on Your Strengths.* Minneapolis: Life Innovations, 2000.

Ősz-Farkas, Ernő (ed.). *Egészségügyi szolgálatok kézikönyve*. Budapest: ESZO, 2003.

Patton, John; Childs, Brian H. *Generationsübergreifende Ehe- und Familienseelsorge*. Göttingen: Vandenhoeck & Ruprecht, 1995.

Pál, Ferenc. *A függőségtől az intimitásig. Vágy, élmény, kapcsolat*. Budapest: Kulcslyuk, 2010.

Peck, M. Scott. *The Road Less Travelled*. New York, New York: Touchstone, 2003.

Peters, Robert W.; Lederer, Laura J.; Kelly, Shane. 'The Slave and the Porn Star: Sexual Trafficking and Pornography.' *Journal of Human Rights and Civil Society*, 2012/5.

Rogers, Carl R. *Partnerschule: Zusammenleben will gelernt sein – das offene Gespräch mit Paaren und Ehepaaren*. München: Kindler, 1975.

Roth, Kornelius. *Sexsucht: Krankheit und Trauma im Verbogenen*. Berlin: Christoph Links, 2004. Third edition.

Rutter, Peter. *Sex in the Forbidden Zone. When Men in Power – Therapists, Doctors, Clergy, Teachers, and Others – Betray a Woman's Trust*. New York, New York: Fawcett Crest, 1991.

Seventh-day Adventist Minister's Handbook. Silver Spring, Maryland: Ministerial Association of The General Conference of Seventh-day Adventists, 1997.

Skrabski, Árpád; Kopp, Mária. *A boldogságkeresés útjai és útvesztői a párkapcsolatokban*. Budapest: Szent István Társulat, 2010.

Sternberg, Robert I. (ed.). *Psychology of Love*. New Haven: Yale University Press, 1988.

Szilágyi, Vilmos. *Nyitott házasság, korszerűbb életstílus*. Budapest: Idegenforgalmi Propaganda és Kiadó Vállalat, 1988.

The ICD-10 Classification of Mental and Behavioural Disorders. Geneva: World Health Organisation, 1994.

Thilo, Hans-Joachim. *Ehe ohne Norm?* Göttingen: Vandenhoeck & Ruprecht, 1978.

Vansteenwegen, Alfons; Luyens, Maureen. *Hoe overleef je een liefdesrelatie*. Kasteelstraat: Lannoo, 209.

Von Schlippe, Arist; Schweitzer, Jochen. *Lehrbuch der systemischen Therapie und Beratung*. Göttingen: Vandenhoeck & Ruprecht, 1997. Third edition.

Webster's Encyclopedic Unabridged Dictionary of the English Language. Avenel: Gramercy Books, 1996.

Willi, Jürg. *Ko-Evolution: Die Kunst gemeinsamen Wachsens*. Reinbek bei Hamburg: Rowohlt, 1985.

Willi, Jürg. *Was hält Paare zusammen? Der Prozeß des Zusammenlebens in psycho-ökologischer Sicht*. Reinbek bei Hamburg: Rowohlt, 1991.

Willi, Jürg. *Die Zweierbeziehung: Spannungsursachen – Störungsmuster – Klärungsprozesse – Lösungsmodelle*. Reinbek bei Hamburg: Rowohlt, 1975.